JOHN McNALLY

BOXING'S FORGOTTEN HERO

First published in 2008 by
Appletree Press Ltd
The Old Potato Station
14 Howard Street South
Belfast BT7 1AP

Tel: +44 (0) 28 90 24 30 74
Fax: +44 (0) 28 90 24 67 56
Email: reception@appletree.ie
Web: www.appletree.ie

Design © Appletree Press, 2008
Text © Barry Flynn, 2008
Photographs © John McNally Collection except where acknowledged

A catalogue record for this book is available from the British Library.

John McNally – Boxing's Forgotten Hero

ISBN: 978 1 84758 093 1

Desk and Marketing Editor: Jean Brown
Copy-editor: Jim Black
Designer: Stuart Wilkinson
Production Manager: Paul McAvoy

9 8 7 6 5 4 3 2 1

AP3565

JOHN McNALLY

BOXING'S FORGOTTEN HERO

BARRY FLYNN

Appletree Press

Dedication by John McNally

To my loving mother Maisie, who, should she have lived, would have been so proud of my achievements, and to my young brother Tomás McNally, who was sadly taken from us before he would know the love of his family.

Forever young, forever young, may you stay forever young.
– Bob Dylan

Dedication by Barry Flynn

To Katrina, Meabh and Deirbhile

CONTENTS

ACKNOWLEDGEMENTS

BY JOHN MCNALLY

In looking back over my life it is truly impossible to name everyone who inspired me along the way. However, I must mention my beloved family who have been my towers of strength for so long. My late father and brother, George and George Jr, were with me every step of the way, my five sisters and of course my Grandmother Rose McCaffrey provided me with so much love and kindness.

The people of the old Pound Loney were an inspiration to us all as they strived in adversity, and I wish to thank the members of St Peter's CYMS for everything they did for me over the years. I would acknowledge those whose tireless dedication to boxing helped me – especially the coaches at the Immaculata, St Mary's and the Star boxing clubs. However, a special mention must go to Sammy Wallace, a true gentleman who inspired me and perfected my skills at the White City boxing club. To the late Sammy Cosgrove, I would record my deepest gratitude for everything. To my long-time friend Mr Liam Nolan, I express my heart-felt thanks for penning so eloquently the foreword to this book. To Liam Burns and Eamon McCartan, I wish to place on the record my thanks for helping keep my name and achievements alive in the collective folk memory.

To the author Barry Flynn, and the staff of Appletree Press, I wish to record my genuine thanks and add that it has been a privilege to be afforded an opportunity to put my story in print.

FOREWORD

BY LIAM NOLAN

When John McNally contacted me by telephone and asked me if I would write the foreword to this biography, a thousand memories flooded back. John and I were born in the same year, and I grew up immersed in boxing, its lore, its language, even its smells – the pungent tang of wintergreen, sweat, and old leather and canvas.

The big difference was that whereas John became a superlative amateur boxer, I, for the very short time I was a participating member of Cobh Amateur Boxing Club, became a very terrible novice with a nose which had a highly developed propensity to bleed if merely looked at. And I was afraid of the sight of blood.

That Harry Macrossan, the white-sweatered stiff-backed little former P.T.I. who was the club trainer didn't tell me to get lost was probably due to the fact that my father was Secretary of the Club, was a qualified referee/judge, a member of both the County Board and the Munster Council of the I.A.B.A., a delegate to the Central Council in Dublin, and had officiated at the European Championships when they were held in Dublin.

Harry, I suspect, had too much respect for my Dad to risk humiliating him by telling him that his eldest son was 'the pits', as far as boxing potential went.

But I loved the history of boxing, and was fascinated by the language. At a very early age I learned about uppercuts, clinches, straight lefts, hooks, crosses, combinations, counter punches, solar plexus punches, the target area, hitting with the knuckle part of the glove, bobbing and weaving, ducking, slipping a punch, jabbing, hooking off the jab, parrying, blocking, feinting, leading, ringcraft. I loved learning the techniques.

At some stage, after listening enthralled for years to Raymond Glendenning and Stewart MacPherson on the BBC, with W. Barrington Dalby doing the inter-round summaries ("Come in, Barry"), I determined that one day I would become a boxing commentator – and I did, and had the honour of Barry Dalby working alongside me.

I'd grown up with the names of Ireland's early European Champions Jimmy Ingle, Paddy Dowdall, Gearoid O'Colmain and Maxie McCullagh ringing in my ears, and grew to love reading about the old-time bare-knuckle breed, men such as James Figg, the first champion, Tom Cribb ('The Black Diamond'), William 'Bendigo' Thompson, Tom Hickman ('The Gaslight Man'), Daniel Mendoza, Tom Molineaux, Jem Belcher, Henry 'Hen' Pearce ('The Game Chicken'), John Gulley, 'Deaf' James Burke, and Jack Broughton ('The Father of the English School of Boxing'). And reading, too, about the later great champions – John L. Sullivan, James J. Corbett, Jack Johnson, Dempsey, Tunney, and so many more.

After John McNally rang, the names came tumbling down the years to me – 'Philadelphia' Jack O'Brien, Battling Levinsky, Battling Siki and, from further down the weight scale, Stanley Ketchel, Mickey Walker, 'Mysterious' Billy Smith, Dixie Kid, George 'Kid' Lavigne, Australian Billy Murphy, Young Griffo, Battling Battalino, 'Bombardier' Billy Wells, Henry Armstrong, 'Pedlar' Palmer, Jimmy Wilde, Fidel LaBarba…

"But you must always remember," my father used to say to me, "those fellows were professional fighters; they took part in fights, they were part of the fight game, which is more a dirty business than a sport. Amateur boxers take part in bouts, and amateur boxing is a contest of skills for points."

He was a purist, my Dad.

Pressing my personal 'fast-forward button' I come to 1952, the year of the Helsinki Olympics, the year in which a small country of just four million people hosted the Games, which they had first hoped to stage back in 1940 but which had been postponed because of World War II. Ireland's Lord Killanin was elected in 1952 to the International Olympic Committee. It was the 'Year of John McNally'.

It was only when I read the first draft of Barry Flynn's fine book that I was reminded of the complicated and (for John McNally) frustrating background to the young Belfast boxer's eventual selection to fill the Bantamweight slot on Ireland's boxing team.

I knew nothing of the Belfast in which John was born and brought up, and the book brings to life the Pound Loney area in which the McNally family lived in one of the small houses on Cinnamond Street. It was a tough area at a tough time, and poverty was endemic. But it was also a time and a place characterised by closeness and laughter in the midst of struggle.

We get informative glimpses of family life and school life, and John's first contact with boxing through the Immaculata Youth Club, and his progress from there to St Mary's, and ultimately to White City.

But it was in the ring in Helsinki that John McNally's finest hour came. Many objective observers and reporters held that he was 'robbed' in the final of the Bantamweight division, when he was on the wrong end of a split decision which gave the verdict to the Finnish boxer Hämäleinen. It seemed beyond doubt that it was the equivalent of professional boxing's 'home-town decision', and that it was given to ensure that the host country ended up with at least one gold medal. Rough justice for the Belfast boxer, the sweet smell of success for the Finn.

But in winning the Silver Medal, John McNally made Irish sporting history by becoming the first Irish boxer to win an Olympic medal of any colour. He was a hero.

When I read of his triumphant return to a rainy Belfast after the Helsinki Olympic Games, I was inevitably reminded of the heart-penetrating simplicity of A.E. Housman's seven short verses named 'To An Athlete Dying Young':

> *The time you won your town the race*
> *We chaired you through the market-place;*
> *Man and boy stood cheering by,*
> *And home we brought you shoulder-high.*
>
> …
>
> *Smart lad to slip betimes away*
> *From fields where glory does not stay*
> *And early though the laurel grows*
> *It withers quicker than the rose.*
>
> …

And further on come those deeply touching lines:

> *Now you will not swell the rout*
> *Of lads that wore their honours out,*
> *Runners whom renown outran*
> *And the name died before the man.*

John McNally is still with us, and his name has not died. But he is, as the title of the book says, a forgotten hero. It doesn't have to be that way, and he doesn't have to remain one of the uncelebrated.

He brought honour to his country, to his native city of Belfast, to the Pound Loney – to all of us.

It is right to cherish sporting heroes, and this book does just that.

Liam Nolan,
Co. Galway

PREFACE

There was a time, in the early 1950s, when John McNally was the biggest thing to hit Ireland since the invention of Penicillin. The nineteen-year-old from the Pound Loney area of Belfast was big news in his native city and in every corner of the island. The reason was that he had quite simply made sporting history. In the wet summer of 1952, McNally won a silver medal at the Helsinki Olympic Games as a bantamweight boxer. Whether it should have been a gold medal or not is explored further in this book, but the simple fact was that he had broken the mould and put Irish amateur boxing on the sporting map.

On his arrival back in his native Belfast, the city came to a virtual standstill as he was paraded around the streets in the driving rain. Fan mail arrived by the bagful at his Cinnamond Street home, and he became a celebrity in his own right. Award shows, beauty contests and prestigious events all became part and parcel of the social life of John McNally. Boxing arenas across Ireland would be packed if McNally's name was added to a bill. He had a fantastic fighting style, with a powerful punch that lit up the amateur scene. In 1953 he followed his Olympic feat by claiming a bronze medal at the European championships in Warsaw – he collapsed through exhaustion after his semi-final. In June of that year, he fought for Europe in the United States against the American Golden Gloves champions and returned undefeated. All was looking fantastic and McNally was truly the golden boy of Irish sport. That, however, is when things started to go wrong.

John McNally maintains that the biggest mistake he ever made in boxing was to turn professional. The paid fight game is no respecter of Olympic medals or impressive pedigrees. McNally soon found that the relatively clean world of the amateur game was a world away from the dog-eat-dog world of professional fighting. Seasoned journeymen were the order of the day and their craft and guile – as well as the bending of the Queensberry Rules – all came to the fore as McNally became lost in the mire of professional boxing. John was to learn the hard way that there are no friends in the professional boxing ring. In reality, boxers are only as good as their last performance in the paid ranks.

Eventually, reality began to bite for John McNally as his career nosedived and in 1960, at the age of twenty-eight, he was finished with the fight game. He was washed-up, married with kids and bitter with a sport that had lapped him up and then spat him out. The achievements of Helsinki were in turn lost in the mists of time and McNally's life returned to the mundane.

Despite this, the name of John McNally is etched forever into the pages of Irish sporting history. The Ireland he represented was a poor nation trying to establish itself on the world's stage. There were no lucrative deals or endorsement opportunities for John McNally on his return from the Olympics, just the prospect of a job as a motor mechanic. There was no grand plan laid out to capitalise on his achievements, and he was left to wander aimlessly through the paid ranks.

This book is a tribute to John McNally. It provides a glimpse into a world long gone. It is a story of a sport that will love a person one day and destroy them the next. It is also a long overdue account of a historic moment in Irish sport. A moment that was to inspire eight further boxers from this island to follow in McNally's footsteps and claim Olympic medals.

PROLOGUE

HELSINKI, SATURDAY 2 AUGUST 1952

The fight is won or lost far away from the witnesses.
— Muhammad Ali

At ten minutes to eight on a balmy August evening in 1952, John McNally's moment of sporting truth finally arrived. As he stood in his corner, tired but enjoying the contented anticipation of Olympic boxing glory, he was rehearsing in his mind the moment when his arm would be raised in victory and history made. Backslaps and knowing winks had been exchanged with his seconds, while in the opposite corner, Finland's great hope, Pentti Hämäläinen, seemed less sure of his chances of gold. For both men, years of dedication would come down to the decision of three judges: an American, an Englishman, and an Austrian. In a simple world, all would be a mere formality. However, this was the Olympic Games, and things were about get very complicated.

In the corner of his eye, the nineteen-year-old Irish bantamweight champion began to notice that the officials were checking and rechecking the judges' cards. Doubt was now creeping into his mind, and in the thoughts of the Irish contingent. Other officials were busy organising the presentation ceremony, while the partisan home crowd began to stamp their feet and become restless. After what seemed like an eternity, the two protagonists were called to the centre of the ring, where both boxers' wrists were gripped tightly by the referee. The outcome of nine minutes of all-out action was now in the lap of the gods. For John McNally and Pentti Hämäläinen, their time had finally arrived. The arena held its collective breath.

The master of ceremonies spoke quickly in his native Finnish, then French, Spanish and finally English. The small Irish band present followed the translations as best they could but, the longer the announcer spoke, the less confident they became that a gold medal was going back home. Suddenly, there was a pause in the proceedings – the moment had arrived. After a pregnant and silent pause, the arena erupted as a massive roar signalled the beginnings of a huge celebration. John McNally's arm was left lifeless and hanging limp. The Finn had been awarded the decision, all was now in slow motion and the crowd was delirious. On the final day of the Helsinki Olympic Games, the host nation had achieved boxing gold by the narrowest of split decisions. Like a little lost boy in the eye of a storm, John McNally had a thousand thoughts in his head as he felt the first tears in a day of many well up in his eyes. With a look of despair, he turned to his corner, but they could not change what the judges had decreed. The decision was final. Absolute. Irreversible. In the celebrating arena, a 'terrible beauty' had indeed been born.

That moment is seared painfully into John McNally's mind. Periodically it comes back to haunt and, maybe, taunt him. He had been standing on the threshold of history and glory, only to see his dream shattered by a split decision. Yet, his feat was momentous as he became Ireland's first-ever Olympic boxing medallist and Northern Ireland's first-ever Olympic medal winner. He lit the flame for those who followed in his wake, especially the four Irish pugilists who took medals in Melbourne in 1956. That day in August 1952 is now history, but John's name will never be erased from the annals of Irish sporting greats. His story is one that has been seldom told – the story of an era long gone, where poverty, determination in adversity and no lack of ambition characterised the greats of the sport of boxing. In 1952, the Belfast boy was merely a 'Cinderella Man', a bit part actor in Finland's boxing glory. However, it all could have been so, so different.

This is the story of John McNally, Ireland's first Olympic boxing medallist.

EARLY DAYS IN THE POUND LONEY

For he comes, the human child,
To the waters and the wild,
With a faery, hand in hand,
From a world more full of weeping than he can understand.

from 'The Stolen Child', W.B. Yeats

The Pound Loney district of Belfast has now largely disappeared from the physical landscape of the city, but not from its collective folk memory. Originally an area set aside by the city fathers for the impounding of stray cattle and other such miscreants, the Pound became settled with mainly Catholic migrants from throughout Ulster as Belfast grew in industrial importance during the Victorian era. Nestled uneasily at the foot of the Falls Road, the nationalist people of the Pound lived cheek-by-jowl with the adjacent and staunchly loyalist Sandy Row. The animosity between the two areas erupted into open sectarian warfare on many occasions during the nineteenth century. The Saltwater – now Boyne – Bridge, where the two districts met, was the scene of many pitched and bloody battles as the sectarian tensions which blighted Belfast erupted in full-scale violence.

The Pound was an area that produced many great characters from within its vibrant streets, but it was also a place that never suffered fools gladly. It was a harsh location to live and survive in, which by the beginning of the twentieth century had evolved into a myriad of close-knit, red-bricked terraced streets. Whilst the linen industry provided work for most of the female population in the district, there was no similar level of employment for the menfolk. As a consequence, poverty, scarcity, and endless struggle characterised the lives of the vast majority of families. Despite the starkness of daily life, the Pound Loney was renowned for its humour and toughness, as well as its tight-knit sense of community, unified in a collective quest to make ends meet.

The period surrounding the partition of Ireland in 1921 saw some of the most vicious sectarian outrages ever perpetrated in Belfast. The Pound Loney was caught in the midst of the violence and this turbulent period partly contributed to the heightened sense of community within the district. The state of Northern Ireland was born in 1921, and an uneasy peace eventually returned to the city. By the early 1930s the main consideration for Belfast citizens was to make a decent living in the face of the devastating economic Depression. In the mean back streets, poverty was still very prevalent and dictated the daily life of the city's inhabitants.

John McNally, the first child born to George and Maisie McNally, entered the world in Belfast's Jubilee Maternity Hospital on Thursday 3 November 1932. Born the very same day in the Co. Roscommon town of Roosky, future Taoiseach Albert Reynolds would go on to play a pivotal role in the Irish peace process. It was also the week that saw Franklin D. Roosevelt elected to the Oval Office in the United States, when he defeated President Herbert Hoover by a virtual landslide. In June of that year, Catholic Ireland had welcomed the International Eucharistic Congress to Dublin, in what was one of the largest manifestations of religious fervour ever witnessed on the island.

In Belfast, two weeks after John's birth, the official opening of the Parliament Buildings took place at Stormont. The imposing edifice made of Portland stone signalled a new Unionist confidence in the future of Northern Ireland. However, the opulence of Stormont was in sharp contrast to the reality of life and daily grind of the vast majority of the citizens of Belfast. The year 1932 was also a year of division and rioting on the streets, as most of the traditional industries, including linen and shipbuilding went into decline. Unemployment was rife and serious rioting – which for the first and only time in Belfast's history united briefly both Protestants and Catholics – occurred as the inadequate nature of the Poor Law relief became a cause for all the poor of the city.

The McNally family lived at No. 13 Cinnamond Street in the middle of the Pound Loney, in a traditional two-up, two-down house in which scarcity was a fact of life. The area was dominated by the spires of St Peter's Catholic Cathedral, from where the monotonous regiment of streets spread out towards the south and west of the city. George McNally worked at a number of menial jobs to keep the family of five daughters and two sons solvent, while Maisie was a devoted homemaker who catered for the whims of their growing family. Living just around the corner from the McNallys was their ever-generous grandmother, Rose McCaffrey, whose kindness and love for John was evident for all to see. As was traditional in the area at the time, Rose provided accommodation for two of the McNally daughters, which helped address the overcrowding in Cinnamond Street. Despite the hardships, John McNally's memories of the Pound Loney are fond.

"We were like everyone else in the area in that we were poor, but there were families worse off than us. The houses were built for the linen industry and very soon they were seen to be too small for the size of the families who lived in the Pound. I recall that my father worked very hard, and he always talked about the time when he worked in the shipyard, putting red lead onto the boats and he always hated that job,

19

as it was so dangerous and dirty. My granny Rose was just special to me as she looked after me and I was the apple of her eye, she was just wonderful. I also recall that there was great laughter in the area, and some great characters that were an inspiration at that time."

In 1936, John entered the local St Comgall's primary school on nearby Divis Street. Three years later, on 3 September 1939, war between Britain and Germany was declared. The wide-eyed pupils of Mr Quinn's class were told the following morning of the historic declaration. However, it was more in excitement than fear that the children greeted the news. Belfast was an important strategic outpost for the war effort and during the opening years of the conflict the citizens had been provided with fabulous displays of derring-do by the legendary Spitfire planes. However, it was felt that the German Luftwaffe was incapable of attacking the city since it was considered to be too far away. That false sense of security was exposed cruelly on the night of Easter Tuesday 15 April 1941, when the city bore the brunt of a devastating Luftwaffe attack.

On the afternoon of the attack, spectators at an Irish League game involving Linfield and Distillery noticed a Junkers plane circling high over Windsor Park. It was in fact a German scouting plane, making a final check on the city in advance of the firestorm that would visit that night. Later, two hundred bombers left their bases in Northern France and in the Low Countries bound for Belfast. By 10.30 that night, the city's air-raid sirens were signalling approaching danger, but this time it was not to be a false alarm.

Under a full moon, wave after wave of unchallenged bombers dropped their incendiaries, high explosives and landmines on the defenceless city. The citizens of Belfast thought that Armageddon had arrived as the onslaught increased in ferocity. By early morning the entire area seemed to be in flames, as a request for assistance to put out the fires was sent to the southern authorities. By the time the attack had ended, almost 1,000 lives had been lost as well as mass swathes of terraced houses in the devastated city. Temporary morgues were established to prepare the dead and mass graves were dug in both the Milltown and City Cemeteries, where the unclaimed bodies were buried. As John McNally recalled, the population of Belfast did not know whether to run to the hills or stay in their beds.

"There was talk that the Germans would get to Belfast but it never really was something that you worried about. On the night of the attack, I remember that there was great excitement, and my mother and father woke us out of bed and took us under the stairs, where we clung together with a mattress over us for protection. We heard the explosions in the distance but there was not really any sense of panic that I recall. It was only when Percy Street on the other side of the Falls Road took a direct hit did we really get frightened.

"The following night saw a mass evacuation from Belfast and we went up to the Falls Park, where there were literally thousands of people sleeping out in the open. I remember that our family slept in a bus in the nearby depot and sure enough there was a second attack. For many nights after that we slept in the open until it was felt safe enough to return to the Loney. I always remember the scenes of devastation in and around the city after that, and knowing that an awful lot of people had been tragically killed. As we were kids we just couldn't understand the whole thing and it was just another part of growing up, but it was horrific looking back on it now."

One of the outcomes of the German onslaught on Belfast saw the authorities introduce a policy of evacuating children from the city to more secure areas in the country. John McNally and his beloved mother Maisie, together with his brother and five sisters, were given lodgings in a farmhouse on land owned by the Graham family in Glenarriff, one of the nine famous Glens of Antrim. The escape from Belfast to one of Ireland's most beautiful areas was a great experience for the McNallys and John's schooling continued in the local town of Waterfoot.

"All it did was rain," he recalled. *"It was a truly lovely place to escape to and every Friday was special, as my father used to come to stay with us, and the farm was just an excellent place for a young lad like me to be at that time."*

As the threat from the Luftwaffe receded, the McNallys eventually returned to Belfast where now the Spitfires could now be seen on daily manoeuvres over the city. However, John McNally soon had other difficulties to face as he entered his teenage years in the Pound Loney.

The McNally family was one where the females held sway and where the menfolk knew their place. John McNally had five sisters, one devoted grandmother, and his mother Maisie looking after him. Sometimes he could play one off against the other, and if he had a disagreement with his mother he 'ran away' to his grandmother's house in the next street and she was able to provide a comforting shoulder. Life was simple, and having his mother and grandmother close provided security in uncertain times.

In early 1945, Maisie McNally travelled the short distance to the Mater Hospital where she gave birth to a third son, who was to be christened Tomás. However, all was not well as the medical staff discovered that Maisie had cancer of the womb. She was transferred to the cancer ward while the infant Tomás was brought home a couple of days later, to be looked after initially by John's aunt, Mary Draine. Maisie McNally's condition worsened, but the children were kept in the dark when they asked about their mother's whereabouts. For John it was nothing to get upset about, as he was assured constantly that she would be home 'in a few days'. Days became weeks and George McNally was a constant visitor to his wife's bedside as she fought to regain health.

Up until quite recently, in most areas of Ireland, there was always a family in a neighbourhood who undertook the duties associated with washing and preparing the dead for a traditional wake. In the Pound Loney area this ritual of 'laying out a body' fell to a woman by the name of Maggie Wright. One morning in August 1945, she knocked on the McNallys' door in Cinnamond Street as the bearer of bad news. John answered the door to be asked whether his mother was home from the hospital and, if not, at what time she was expected to return. A mood of joyful expectation was soon shattered when it was explained to John that his mother's return was not going to be a happy occasion, as she had passed away that morning.

"I was stunned into silence, as I still believed that she wasn't really ill and would be home any day. I just couldn't understand what had happened and then my sisters started to cry and wail as it was related to us that she died of cancer, but I was too young to understand such things. All I knew was that my mother had died, and I just felt so lonely and full of despair. Times were different back then and people were just expected to cope, but I remember in the weeks after her death that I could hear my father cry himself to sleep, and this continued for many months. We were all shattered by the experience but nobody wanted to talk about it, and we were just expected to survive. We were no different to other families in the district as death was a way of life, but when it hit us, it hit us bad. My mother was a beautiful woman with long red hair. It left an awful void in my life and it was my granny who in some ways filled that emptiness, even though she was suffering also."

Soon after the death of John's mother, a distraught Mary Draine visited the home of Granny Rose in Crane Street. She was inconsolable as she related to John's grandmother a terrible dream she had had where Maisie McNally returned from the dead to speak with her. Still shaken, she told Rose of how Maisie had told her that she was broken hearted and longed to have youngest child Tomás back with her. Mary was consoled and told to go home to look after the child as he needed her.

The infant Tomás took a chest infection and died soon after, aged only five months. For John McNally, it was then that sport became the escape that helped him cope in difficult times. Sadly, neither Maisie nor young Tomás McNally would witness the glory that lay ahead for John.

BOXING AS A WAY OF LIFE

See Belfast, devout, profane and hard.
from 'Valediction', Louis MacNeice

As the war ended, an institution was established near to the Pound Loney which was to provide an invaluable sporting escape for the youth of the area. The Immaculata Youth Club had originally been founded in 1944 by the Legion of Mary Society in Belfast's Corn Market. The initial aim of the club had been to work with children who had been released from borstal in an attempt to provide an alternative lifestyle through sport. After a year, the club left the centre of Belfast and re-located to Devonshire Street in the Lower Falls, where it opened its doors to all the children of the vicinity. The two main sports offered by the Immaculata were boxing and soccer, although table tennis and other pursuits were available to the members. The club acted like a magnet to the youth of the area, and it was natural that John McNally would be attracted to the boxing scene.

Street fighting and fisticuffs were a way of life for most of the boys of the Pound Loney. Different streets had their own squads and John ran with his friends from English Street, who were enemies with the youths from the adjacent Bow, Scotch and Baker Streets. Whilst the scrapes were never too serious, it was the habit of coming off second best that led John to the Immaculata.

"I was too stubborn in fights. I was always getting the worst, so when a friend of mine called Patsy Monaghan suggested that we join the boxing club I just jumped at the chance," recalled John. "On my first evening at the club the trainer Tommy Madine put the gloves on Patsy and me, and put us in the ring where we just went for it. It was a tremendous release, and Tommy was eyeing us to see if we had any natural talent. I was hooked and began to take the game seriously and trained religiously every night. Boxing was a great escape for me at the time. I was young and the death of my mother was still hurting, but I began to concentrate on the boxing as a means of coping. My grandmother Rose had become a second mother to me, and she was to mentor me throughout my career."

Within a few months, John came under the tutelage of a trainer called Willie Holden who was, to say the least, a hard taskmaster. Holden was a perfectionist whose style was demanding on the young pugilists. He drove the boys to the extreme, and his exacting methods sometimes were resented by the boxers. One of his habits was to call up to the boys' houses and ridicule those who chose to stay at home doing schoolwork, as opposed to attending the club.

The standards set by Holden had an immediate effect however, and, in 1946, John qualified for the Ulster final of the 5 stone 7lb juvenile class. His opponent in the Ulster Hall that evening was a boxer by the name of Paddy Graham, who would go on to carve out an impeccable career in the ring. The fight that night was a battle from the first to the last bell and Graham was adjudged to be the winner. Undeterred, John decided to enter the all-Ireland championships where the prospect of an early rematch with Graham was on the cards. As it turned out, the Ulster champion was beaten in the quarter-final by an up-and-coming prospect called 'Spike' McCormick and John was to claim the national title by then defeating Holy Family's Louis Watson. As the Immaculata's first Irish champion, John became a local star and other advantages were soon to come his way.

Gerry and Joe Baker were brothers who were involved in the running of the Immaculata club. They held a bit of sway in the community and one evening they called to see John, who was recuperating at home after having his tonsils removed. At that stage, John was still a pupil at St Comgall's school and the brothers suggested that his education could benefit if they could arrange a transfer of the Christian Brothers' school in Hardinge Street, which they could organise. Such a transfer offered John a curriculum which included science, metalwork, English, maths, a language and, of course, religion. As expected, he jumped at the chance to move to Hardinge Street, where Brothers McGuinness, Dwane and Burgess amongst others, began to hone John's academic skills.

One of the biggest events to have occurred in the Falls Road took place in 1946 when the film crews descended en masse to film parts of the Carol Reed epic *Odd Man Out*. The film starred James Mason, as a character called Johnny McQueen who was trying to escape from the police after a badly organised bank robbery. For boys in the area the excitement surrounding the movie only reinforced ambitions of travel and fame.

At this stage, John McNally was dedicating himself to his flourishing boxing career. However, he had left the Immaculata and moved to the St Mary's club in nearby King Street as a disagreement occurred in the Devonshire Street club. At the centre of the dispute was trainer Willie Holden: he left the club and took with him a number of the better prospects, including John McNally. The Immaculata were none too pleased to lose their star boxers. The Ulster Council was called in to mediate in the dispute, but John McNally would never return to the Immaculata. The St Mary's club honed John's skills further and he went from strength to strength, becoming quite a draw at local shows.

"Willie Holden always said that I was a natural boxer and I suppose I stayed with him as he had brought me so far. I recall that we were

boxing twice, sometimes three times, on a Sunday night at various clubs across Belfast," John recalled.

"We started off at the Immaculata and all the boys were given an ice-cream from the local parlour for taking part, which was a big treat back then. We then ran to the St George's club for another scrap, and they would have lemonade on offer. However, the biggest treat for me came at St Mary's, when we would be rewarded with apple pie that had been baked by my sisters. The fact was that these treats were the best thing you could have given the boys as, let's face it, we were always hungry and you can't eat medals for supper."

In 1947, John again won the Ulster juvenile crown, this time at 6 stone, but a trip to Dublin for the all-Ireland series was not something that gained the approval of the Brothers at Hardinge Street. Brother McGuinness ruled the roost in the school, and when he heard that John was not concentrating on studying for his examinations, he decided to put a stop to it. One morning in February, McGuinness called John into his office to discuss his boxing career. John's leaving examinations were the main priority for the Christian Brother; when he discovered that his pupil had fought the previous evening, he forbade him to box until after he left school. Father McAlea, the chaplain of the St Mary's club, tried to intercede on John's behalf, but it was to no avail as McGuinness was adamant in his decision. Despite this setback, John continued to train and fight in non-championship bouts, against the ruling of Brother McGuinness. John's fitness was something that marked him out and gave him the added edge over opponents.

One of the most forward-looking clubs in Belfast in the 1940s was the White City club, based in York Street. Under trainer Sammy Wallace the club was setting the highest standards and John McNally was naturally impressed. One evening, in the ring with an up-and-coming star of the White City called Arthur McGill, John was caught by one of the sweetest left hooks he ever had the privilege to receive. That bout led John to believe that he would better himself at the White City where pugilists such as Tom Walsh were setting the standards in Irish boxing.

Sammy Wallace was to become the greatest influence on John McNally's career. Once he had made the decision to leave St Mary's, it was natural that he would form a winning alliance with Wallace. Although the White City trainer had no pedigree in the boxing ring, he had a devotion to game and had picked up some valuable experience in the United States. His methods and knowledge were far in advance of anything in Belfast at that time, and he soon worked on perfecting any flaws in McNally's style.

"Sammy was a coach and not a trainer, and there is a very subtle difference," recalled John. *"I first met him in Dublin at a tournament and he impressed me the way he handled his boxers and how they performed. In many ways, he was too nice a man to be in the boxing game, but the way he taught me was second-to-none. He was a master of the art of ring craft and how to ghost and move. He taught me how to punch hard and move fast, how to use the ropes and slide. Technically, there was nobody in Ireland at that time who could touch him. My game improved immensely and it was in 1947 that I began to believe that I could make it to the top in the amateur game."*

In 1948, John McNally left the Christian Brothers' to take up an apprenticeship as a mechanic at the Belfast firm Isaac Agnew. In that year a great sporting event whetted McNally's appetite for competitive sport at the highest level. London, which had been due to host the 1944 Olympic Games, was the venue for the XIV Olympiad. Those Games were the first to receive mass media coverage, and athletes representing 60 nations took part. The Olympics were a triumph for Britain, as London was still recovering from the devastations of the war. Wembley Stadium was fitted with a temporary running track, and was used as the main athletics stadium. The major star of the Games was the Dutch runner Fanny Blankers-Koen, who won gold in four events and became an instant hero. The carnival of sport was carried in every cinema, newspaper and radio station. For a fifteen-year-old fledgling boxer in Belfast's Cinnamond Street, the Olympic Games were now the ultimate sporting dream to which he could aspire.

With John McNally now based at the White City club, the Olympic Games held in London in 1948 would set in motion a train of events that would eventually see him travel to the XV Olympic Games in Helsinki in 1952.

STEPPING UP TO THE MARK

Make your hay before the fine weather leaves you.
– Proverb

Not that getting to the Olympic Games was going to be easy. However, the key for John McNally was that he began to peak at the right time. More importantly, he came to prominence in the right arena – the National Stadium in Dublin. From 1949, juvenile and then Ulster senior crowns came McNally's way with consummate ease. Significantly, in 1951, McNally took the Ulster – beating Paddy Graham in the final – and Irish junior flyweight crowns. Most notably, he recorded a victory over the British ABA flyweight champion, Welshman Ritchie Jenkins, in a tournament at the Ulster Hall. People were beginning to take notice of the White City boxer, however a trip to an Olympic Games was still a total long shot.

In January 1952 John won the Ulster Senior title at his first attempt, by defeating George O'Neill of the St George's Club at the Ulster Hall. In what was described as the 'surprise of the night' by the *Belfast Telegraph*, McNally's win was reported also as 'brilliant'. Ulster titles were fine and well, but held little clout on the all-Ireland stage. Therefore, the problem for John was to make a mark in the National Stadium in Dublin, where the hometown favourites held sway. One of those favourites was an excellent boxer from the St Francis' Club by the name of Benny Carabini. Among the highlights of the boxing calendar in Dublin was the annual Polikoff's Tournament. Sponsored by the men's outfitters, the crowd attending the National Stadium were assured always that the cream of Irish amateur boxing would be on show.

As reigning Ulster senior champion at bantamweight, McNally was invited as a guest to take part in the tournament against the skilful Carabini. The Dubliner was aiming to establish his credentials as a contender for the Helsinki Games and McNally was seen as a good – but not too difficult – test of his ability. That evening in the arena, a cold Friday night in February, the papers reported that there was almost a revolt among the crowd, but this had nothing to do with the boxing on show. The fact was that the heating had broken down and the punters were literally freezing. Stamping of feet and demands for refunds permeated the smoky and cold air inside the Stadium. Worried officials and members of the Polikoff firm did their best to subdue the cold fans, but it was a most unsatisfactory state of affairs. Eventually, Carabini entered the ring to warm – or should that be cold? – applause. Now was the perfect time for McNally to make his mark by beating a former Irish champion on his home turf: he duly obliged. The *Irish Press* reported on the victory:

> 'The Belfast-man showed exceptional skill in gaining a well-deserved win, for he had a grand right hand and was a much faster puncher…and was on target with every blow.'

In his next Dublin outing, the Arbour Hill tournament in March, John McNally was matched with Paddy Kelty, a short-reach boxer who was favourite to land the bantamweight ticket to Helsinki. Kelty was the reigning Irish champion and had recently dispatched England's Tommy Nicholls with style in an international at the Stadium. He was a seasoned amateur, but McNally had come like a steam train out of the blue, and Kelty was wary of the Ulsterman. Since this contest was seen as a dress rehearsal for the Irish senior final, there was a lot at stake. As it turned out, the fight was a personal triumph for Kelty, but his victory raised more questions about his ability than it answered.

Whilst being awarded the contest, the journalists at ringside considered Kelty as most fortunate. For most of the bout he was forced to stay at the end of McNally's jab and had to employ rushing tactics to score. Under the headline 'Short-reach boxer was lucky to win' the *Irish Independent*'s observer ended his report with a suggestion that a return match would see McNally victorious. Perhaps, with this in mind, Kelty chose to opt out of the Irish Senior Championships in the belief that his initial victory over McNally would put him in the prime spot for the Olympics.

In mid-March, at the finals of the senior championships, the papers were reporting the triumph of McNally and touting him – and featherweight Harry Perry – as future household names. The Belfastman came up against Sandymount's Mick Towers at bantamweight and made short work of the Dubliner. Towers was no pushover – he had beaten some of the top boxers in Ireland – but he had no answer for the speed and power of McNally. Towers ('wisely', according to the *Irish Times*) retired before the end of the second round, and the cup was going north. In the featherweight bout Harry Perry, a seventeen-year-old Terenure schoolboy, beat Tommy Reddy with a display of 'delightful youthful ambition'.

Soon after, Harry Perry was told by officials that he was considered too young to go to the Olympics, and Reddy went in his place. Nineteen-year-old John McNally faced a similar battle. The man who had beaten him a month previously, Paddy Kelty, held all the aces. Despite the result of the Irish final, nothing was resolved as the Games drew near.

WINNING OVER THE SCEPTICS

It's not the dog in the fight; it's the fight in the dog.
— Proverb

It has been said of Irish boxing that more battles are fought outside the ring than have actually taken place within the ropes. The history of the amateur and professional game is littered with fall-outs, together with suggestions of administrative skulduggery that hindered – or even ended – many a promising career. John McNally's progress to the Helsinki Olympics was by no means as smooth as the new Irish champion could have hoped. Despite taking the national title in Dublin in March a question mark hung over his participation in the Games: the Irish Amateur Boxing Association procrastinated over its choice for the bantamweight berth. At merely nineteen years of age, McNally's youth was against him; at 5ft 9in tall, weighing just over 8 stone, he was not thought to possess the body strength to compete in Helsinki. Further proof of his ability was required.

As champion he could argue that he was a natural first choice, yet the authorities dithered, and other names were mooted and suggested as the politics of boxing came to the fore. A considerable body of press opinion held that the champion would not have the ability to cope at the Olympics, and the name being tipped for the spot was, of course, Dublin's Paddy Kelty. This was the same Paddy Kelty who had sat out the Irish championships, which McNally had won. He posed a serious threat to John's ambitions, due to his considerable experience and reputation. In addition, Kelty was a member of the Corinthians Boxing Club, a number of whose members held sway in the Central Committee of the Association. In the interest of all-Ireland balance and harmony, the pressure was on to add Kelty's name to the team – the reigning champion was a mere bit player as the various opinions were aired. It was apparent that a number of crucial tests lay ahead for John McNally if he was prove his class and win over the grandees of the Association's Central Council.

"I recall that I felt that winning the Irish title had been all-too-easy, and I was a bit disappointed that there had not been better competition," recalled John. *"The fact was that my trainer Sammy Wallace had warned me in the ring after I won the title that my battle to prove myself was only beginning. There were people in the IABA* [Irish Amateur Boxing Association] *out there who had no intention of sending me to the Olympic Games. I knew that I had limited experience and perhaps lacked the physique that more experienced boxers had. My waist was only 27 inches and my height gave me the appearance of being there for the taking, so the jury was out as far as the Olympics were concerned. I knew at an early stage that the only way that I could silence my doubters was to beat Kelty in the Stadium, and that was what I resigned myself to doing."*

As Irish champion, John was picked for his first senior international, which was to be against Scotland in Dublin on 29 March. The National Stadium was filled to capacity that night as the Celtic nations clashed for the annual Kuttner Shield. McNally knew that the doubters were watching from the ringside as he faced up to the formidable Scot Tom Beattie in the bantamweight clash. Watching in the wings, waiting to capitalise on any shortcomings that McNally might show, were the trustees of the IABA and the hometown favourite, Paddy Kelty. Despite the pressure, the fight with Beattie was a total triumph for McNally. He knew that the best way to answer his critics was to give an assured and competent performance, which he duly delivered.

Beattie was under pressure from the start as John attacked with stinging lefts, which were followed by pinpoint right hooks. His speed and agility left the Scot bemused as the crowd responded with deafening roars. By the second round, Beattie had received a cut under each eye as McNally's onslaught increased in ferocity. Eventually, with 30 seconds to go, the referee was forced to intervene and lead the dishevelled Scot back to his corner. It was a case of a job well done in the right arena for the Belfast boy. McNally was adjudged in the press to been the star of the evening, as Ireland destroyed the Scots on a 9-1 score line. However, the selectors remained decidedly indifferent when it came to finalising the squad for Helsinki.

The next hurdle John McNally would have to negotiate in his quest for an Olympic place was Ireland's meeting with the formidable might of the New York Golden Gloves champions in Dublin on 25 April. If the nineteen-year-old Belfast boxer had it all to prove, then his meeting with Jake Corvino was the stage on which to do it. Corvino was truly a class act, who hailed from the tough 'Little Italy' area of New York City. In 1951, as a total novice, he saw an article in a local paper which reported that the winners of the New York Golden Gloves Championships would undertake a tour of Europe in 1952 which, most importantly, would include a visit to Italy.

For a first-generation Italian-American, a trip to Italy to see his grandparents was the key to him taking up boxing. Within six months, the inexperienced Corvino was New York Golden Gloves champion, and the trip to Italy was on the cards. He had a vicious punch and his reputation as a brawler was renowned. The pressure was on McNally and it was felt by many that his relative inexperience would be exposed badly by the dangerous Yank. A defeat at Corvino's hands would leave the way open for Kelty to claim the bantamweight spot at Helsinki. Not only did John McNally acknowledge that possibility but the patrons in the National Stadium were acutely aware of this, as the Irish champion entered the ring.

"I remember that I was due to fight an American guy called Hurston, but when I got on the scale the American coach pointed at me and looked over at Jake Corvino and said 'He's yours Jake, go easy on him!' and I knew I was going to be up against a class act. Sure enough when the fight began, he came straight across the ring and hit me with three of the hardest right hands that I have ever taken. I heard the gasps from the crowds in the arena and to this day, I do not know how I stayed on my feet. If he had have hit me a fourth time there is no way that I could have continued as he had me shaken. I survived the onslaught by working my way around the ropes and when I got back to the corner I told Sammy Wallace that I thought that the Stadium was about to collapse around me."

If anything, Wallace had always been a pillar of strength for his protégé, and he calmed him down during the crucial minute he spent with him at the end of the first. In the following two rounds, McNally kept the American at the end of his jab and began to score with uppercuts and hooks. Corvino's right hooks were neutralised by clever defensive boxing, and the crowd began to warm to John as he proceeded to outbox Corvino. In the third round, McNally had the crowd roaring him to victory as he pressed forward and threatened to end the contest. As the bell rang, McNally had learnt a valuable lesson – he would never ever leave himself open to right hooks thrown over his guard. He was improving with every outing. The scalp of Jake Corvino was taken by a unanimous decision, increasing McNally's reputation in Irish boxing. His case for Olympic inclusion was now watertight: it was then placed back in the hands of the Central Council to finalise the team.

On 28 April, the Central Commitee agreed that it would send eight boxers to the Olympics, and forwarded the names of brothers Andrew and Tommy Reddy, Terry Milligan, Peter Crotty, Willie Duggan and John Lyttle to the Irish Olympic Council for approval. Despite McNally's heroics against Corvino, the Commitee again delayed in finalising the name for the bantamweight and lightweight spots. Perhaps they were genuinely concerned at John's youth, but he had excelled in his two international outings and the wait began to affect his confidence. In Dublin, Paddy Kelty's supporters were arguing his case, and the authorities decided that a box-off was the only way that the matter could be resolved. For John McNally, the bar had just been raised again despite the fact that he had more than proved his ability emphatically at international level. It was determined that Paddy Kelty and Belfast's George O'Neill would clash in a semi-final for the right to meet McNally in the final box-off. The lightweight class would see Tony Byrne, Dave Connell, John Cummins and Kevin Martin go head-to-head for the final place.

"It was like banging my head off a brick wall, for it seemed that I had been caught up in all the politics of the Association. There was obviously a significant body of opinion of the view that I should not be picked for the Olympics, and I had to respect their view and go through the trial. The fact is that if you are fit physically then that helps to get you ready mentally, and I was fine in my mind. The win over Corvino left me on top of the world and there was no way that I was going to fail at this stage. I was really confident that I could beat Kelty and I trained like a demon in preparation for that fight. I considered the whole thing to be a distraction as my sights were set on Helsinki."

Sure enough, Kelty was victorious in his bout with O'Neill and the fight with McNally was set for the Stadium on 6 June. With a trip to Helsinki at stake, the contest, which took place in front of a large and partisan Dublin crowd, was a bruising encounter which, in accordance with the rules of natural justice, went the way of McNally, the reigning Irish champion. In the first round, McNally gave Kelty a boxing lesson. Accurate straight left hands caught the Dubliner on numerous occasions and laid the foundations for his success. Kelty, the smaller, stockier boxer, tried to work inside McNally but was met with a barrage of piston-like jabs and there could only be one winner. When the decision was called unanimously in McNally's favour, the emotional Belfast boxer stood vindicated in the ring. Meanwhile, in the lightweight class, Kevin Martin from the Mount Street Club saw off Drogheda's Tony Byrne – who would go on to claim a bronze at Melbourne in 1956 – and so the Central Council retired that evening to finalise the Irish Olympic boxing team.

"That night in the Stadium against Kelty was the first and only time that I ever went into a ring in an angry mood. I had been truly sickened by the way that the whole issue regarding the bantamweight selection had been handled, and I was not going to be beaten. I was fit and determined and knew that there were people out there waiting for me to slip up so as they could justify my exclusion from the Olympics. I boxed immaculately in the first two rounds, and knew that the judges could not deny me as the bell sounded at the end of the bout. Sure enough, I got the decision and it was then that I knew that there was no way that I could be overlooked."

As he showered after the fight, McNally got word that he was to report to the office at the Stadium where the Central Council had been meeting. After his win over Kelty, John had no fear that he was to be overlooked this time and made his way to the office. He duly knocked and entered the office where the President of the Association, Garda Chief Superintendent Paddy Carroll, rose from his chair and shook the victor's hand. He was warm in his congratulations and told John that he had just secured his ticket to Helsinki. Garda Carroll added that the three most important things that John could do now was to keep fit, keep to a strict diet and, most importantly, get his measurements sent down to Dublin in order that his Olympic blazer and trousers could be made.

The following day, John and his father went to the home of Dan Cregan, a tailor from Ross's Street off the Falls Road. By three that afternoon a telegram had been dispatched to Dublin advising the Olympic Association that John's chest measured 40 inches, while his waist was a mere 27 inches.

THE LONG ROCKY ROAD
TO HELSINKI

The one who waits for a fine day will get a fine day.
– Proverb

According to an ancient Greek legend, the Olympic Games were founded by Herakles, one of the sons of Zeus. The first Games for which a written record exists were held in 776BC, where a naked cook from Elis, named Coroebus, won the main event – a sprint known as the Stade. Thus, it is generally accepted in history that Coroebus was the first-ever Olympic champion. In ancient Greece, the Olympic Games were the highlight of the social calendar where each event was considered to be almost sacred. To win an Olympiad was the closest that a mere mortal could come to being considered godlike whilst still living on Earth. In fact, the Games were considered so important that a sacred truce was called throughout Greece, so that the festivities could take place in peace and harmony. All wars stopped and ambassadors negotiated many treaties between feuding cities during the Games. The Games grew in importance throughout Roman times as a means of promoting friendship and goodwill among peoples. A tradition grew of awarding champions with a wreath of olive leaves as a sign of peace and hope. The Games continued for over a millennium until in 393AD a Christian Roman Emperor, Theodosius I, put an end to the event. This was due to their perceived pagan influences, in that they promoted prostitution and other sorts of 'ungodly acts' and vice among the many thousands of spectators – and athletes – that descended on the event. That, as they say, was that for approximately 1500 years, as the notion of the Olympic Games was lost in the mists of time.

In the 1880s a French aristocrat by the name of Pierre de Coubertin instigated a revival of the Olympic ideal. Known as 'Le Rénovateur', de Coubertin was convinced that many of the ills of the French nation were due to a 'lack of vigour' among its general population. After studying the education systems of Britain, Germany and America, he became convinced that sport and exercise were the keys to industrial and military greatness. A scholar of note, Coubertin was aware of the ancient Olympic Games and through endless campaigning, arm-twisting and persuasion, he eventually saw his dream come to reality in Athens in the first week of April 1896. Those Games were a legacy far removed from the celebration of humanity we know today as the Olympics. Contestants did not represent nations as such but were chosen – or invited – to attend at their own expense. Indeed, some contestants were tourists who just happened to be in Greece at the time of the Games.

Ireland's early participants in the Olympic Games saw them compete under the guise of Great Britain whilst the political battles surrounding Home Rule weakened the linkages across the Irish Sea. Historically, the first Irishman to win an Olympic gold medal was John Pius Boland, who won gold medals at both the 1896 tennis singles and doubles events. His feat at the Games in Athens, at a time when competing at the Games was the preserve of the privileged, was monumental in its day. Later, he returned to Ireland where he became a Member of Parliament for the constituency of South Kerry. Boland's achievements were for many years credited as gold medals for Britain, but it is now accepted that his achievements were the first of Ireland's Olympic titles.

Other notable 'Irish' medallists included John Jesus Flanagan who was born in the year 1873 in the town of Kilbreedy, Co. Limerick. In 1897, at the age of twenty-four, he was considered to be the world record holder in the hammer event and in that year, he emigrated to the United States. At the Paris Olympics in 1900, Flanagan, representing the United States, took gold and followed this feat by defending his title easily at the 1904 Games in St Louis. At the London Games of 1908, Flanagan made it a hat trick of gold medals when he beat then-world record holder – and fellow Irish-American – Matt McGrath into second place.

When it came to achievements that were purely 'Irish' in origin, the name of Tom Kiely, who claimed gold in the 'All Round Championship' at the 1904 Games, is considered to have been the most famous. Born in 1869 in the town of Ballyneale, just outside the Co. Tipperary town of Carrick-on-Suir, Kiely's event was the forerunner to the modern-day decathlon. Representing Great Britain, and competing in ten events in one day, his achievement made him an instant superstar in Ireland and beyond.

With Partition in 1921, the island was divided into two entities, namely the Irish Free State and Northern Ireland. However, whilst the border was created, many sporting bodies, including boxing, were still organised on an all-island basis, though in the North sports such as athletics chose to affiliate with Great Britain. In 1924 the International Olympic Committee [IOC] formally recognised the Irish Free State and subsequently Ireland competed in that year's Paris Games. Strangely, the Olympics in those days catered for a wider variety of skills: while the country did not win medals in any of the sporting pursuits, Jack B. Yeats claimed a silver medal for his painting entitled *Swimming*, whilst, in literature, Oliver St John Gogarty claimed bronze for his poem 'Ode to the Tailteann Games'. In boxing, Paddy Dwyer was beaten in the semi-final of the welterweight division by the eventual gold medallist Jean Delarge. However, it was not until 1952 that both beaten semi-finalists in boxing were to be awarded bronze medals, and Dwyer was beaten into fourth place after a box-off for bronze.

In the 1928 Games held in Amsterdam, Ireland claimed a first-ever medal in its own right. The man who took the honours in the hammer event was a Corkman by the name of Dr Pat O'Callaghan. Whilst he travelled – at his own expense – more in hope than expectation, O'Callaghan (whose older brother Con was competing in the decathlon) excelled in his event to beat the English favourite Malcolm Noakes and the Swede Ossian Skiöld. O'Callaghan entered the realm of Olympic greats when he repeated his heroics four years later and took gold in the Los Angeles Games. Those Games were a triumph for Ireland as Bob Tisdall, who was born in 1907 in Ceylon, of Anglo-Irish parentage, claimed gold in the 400 metres hurdles. In his opening heat Tisdall equalled the Olympic record and in the final, despite stumbling at the final hurdle, won the gold medal in a world-record time of 51.7 seconds. The rules in those days stated that if an athlete knocked over a hurdle then the time could not be considered. Tisdall was denied the record, but not the gold.

In 1936, for the first and only time since Independence, Ireland was precluded from taking part in an Olympic Games due to a dispute with the International Amateur Athletic Federation. However, the Berlin Olympic Games were overshadowed by the spectre of Adolf Hitler and the supremacist ideology of Nazi Germany. The Nazis saw the Olympic ideal as further means of promoting their fascist philosophy, and no expense was spared in pursuit of this aim. The Nazi propaganda machine – under the direction of Joseph Goebbels – went into overdrive and the Olympic ideal was tested to the extreme as the Germans excluded Jewish athletes from their team. Despite the threat of a boycott, the United States decided to participate and Jesse Owens became the man who destroyed the supremacist lie by taking four gold medals, to the dismay of the Führer. The onset of World War II meant that no Games were held until a battle-scarred London hosted the Olympics in 1948. Ireland competed but not at athletics, and no medals were won, despite the heroics of boxer Mick McKeon, who lost to Great Britain's John Wright in the semi-final of the middleweight class.

By 1952, Ireland was fighting to establish itself on the world stage as a creditable international entity. The animosity with its neighbour Britain had festered throughout the Second World War as Ireland declared itself neutral, much to the dismay of Winston Churchill and the Stormont Government in the North. The legacy of this falling out was still to the fore as the 'Free State' declared itself a Republic in 1949. Helsinki represented an important departure for the Republic of Ireland as she made her debut on the world stage as a truly independent country.

John McNally, from Belfast in Northern Ireland, was picked to represent the Republic of Ireland. The 1937 Constitution of Ireland laid claim to the whole island of Ireland on behalf of the Irish Free State and the sport of boxing was organised on this basis. Sport and politics in Ireland have always been an uneasy match, but boxing by and large escaped any such controversy. However, at an official level, McNally representing 'a foreign country' created a dilemma. The government and unionist media in the North would toe the political line and concentrate on how the Great Britain team was faring, with McNally's progress warranting a footnote at best. Times have changed in Belfast today, but in 1952 representing Ireland at the Olympic Games was something that was frowned upon by the Northern powers that were.

PLANES, BOATS, TRAINS AND AUTOMOBILES

Tread softly for you tread on my dreams
from "He Wishes For the Cloths of Heaven" W.B. Yeats

The City of Belfast, for somebody approaching it for the first time, is truly a geographical wonder. Built around the mouth of the Farset River at the top of the Lagan Valley, the city spreads out around its wide Lough and is enclosed beautifully between the imposing Black and Divis Mountains on the Co. Antrim side, with the rolling Castlereagh Hills providing a softer image on the Co. Down fringe. Beyond the mountains to the north is the breathtaking sight of the historic Cave Hill and McArt's Fort, with its dramatic basalt cliffs sweeping down towards the Antrim Road. It was here in 1795 that the United Irishmen Theobald Wolfe Tone and Henry Joy McCracken met to swear an oath of rebellion against the English Crown Forces – an act that was to eventually end with both men being sentenced to death three years later after the failure of the 1798 Rebellion.

With such picturesque and historic scenery, steep and punishing gradients, the Belfast hills and mountains provide a perfect backdrop and training ground for any prospective athlete. So it was that John McNally found himself high above the city early each morning as the trip to Helsinki drew ever closer. While the

Pound Loney slept, he rose religiously at 5.30 am to take to the hills and returned only after a 10-mile stretch had been covered on the steep slopes of the Black Mountain. From January until mid-July 1952, this routine had been undertaken religiously by McNally, and this was followed by severe workouts in the evening under Sammy Wallace in the White City gym. Undoubtedly, this austere test of McNally's endurance had helped him through the many trials and tribulations he had encountered to get to the Games. As his fitness levels reached their peak so too did his confidence – being Irish champion on the Olympic stage would count for nothing unless you had an unshakeable belief in your own ability. With two weeks left until the Games, John McNally was peaking physically and with his mind focused and positive, he felt unbeatable.

"Sammy Wallace said to me that I was the Irish bantamweight champion and, as such, should fear nobody as I should treat my opponents as merely champions of their own country – no better than me – and to not listen to anyone who would glorify the boxers who may be there. If I was going to start doubting my own ability before the Games, well, I may as well have stayed in Belfast, Sammy told me. What was happening though was that as I became fitter, my mind became more positive and I began to grow in confidence, which was half the battle."

Belfast had four Olympic representatives in 1952. In athletics, Thelma Hopkins, a mere sixteen-year-old, went to the Games to represent Great Britain in the high jump event. Despite her youth, she finished in a creditable fourth place and would go on to claim a silver medal at the Melbourne Games in 1956. Hopkins would prove herself to be a fine all-round athlete. She went on to break the world high-jump record in Belfast also in 1956, as well as gaining forty caps for Ireland at hockey. However, the political and sporting intricacies of the island of Ireland meant that the three other representatives from the city were boxers in the green of Ireland.

Joining John McNally as Belfast's other boxing representatives in the Irish Olympic team were the light-welterweight champion Terry Milligan and Greencastle heavyweight John Lyttle. Terry, who hailed from the Short and Harland club, was three years older than John, and had established his credentials by taking a bronze medal at the 1951 European Championships, which had taken place in Milan. It was a sure thing to say that Milligan was considered by the media as Ireland's best hope for a medal, with McNally's youth something that the pundits felt that would hinder him on the higher stage.

At heavyweight, standing 5ft 10in was John Lyttle, who it was said had the heart of a lion. In March of that year, at the Ireland versus the New York Golden Gloves Champions bill, Lyttle had the National Stadium on its collective feet as he tore into the heavyweight champion Ed Saunders and threatened to topple the man who would go on to win gold in Helsinki. Lyttle lost that night, but Saunders went to Helsinki with an ambition to avoid Lyttle. The three pugilists all became good friends as the Games approached, and on the morning of Wednesday 9 July 1952 John McNally, John Lyttle and Terry Milligan boarded the Enterprise service from Belfast's Great Victoria Street bound for Dublin to meet up with the Irish team travelling for Finland and the XV Olympiad.

"There was no real big send-off for us in Belfast, but I remember that everybody I met in the Pound wanted to shake my hand and wish me the best of luck. My father and grandmother were very good to me, and they gave me a couple of pounds, but the whole amateur status of the Olympics was something that had to be adhered to strictly at all times, so we did not openly say we had been given anything. The rules at that time said that the athletes could be given two dollars a day spending money from their Associations, but we all had money stashed away going there. I recall that my employer, Mr Isaac Agnew, held an event for me at which he gave me a beautiful wallet, which had a crisp £10

note in it. I was so pleased, as I was losing money by being out of work, and this gesture more than made up for that: and I will never forget that act of kindness from a very good man."

On arriving at Amien Street Station in Dublin, the three boxers made their way across O'Connell Bridge to Moran's Hotel in Exchequer Street, where the rest of the Irish boxers had assembled. There they were met by Irish team managers Frank Cooper and Christy Murphy, who laid down the ground rules on how they were now 'ambassadors for Ireland' and 'expected to behave with the utmost decorum' or else the Olympic Council would send them home in disgrace ('and you wouldn't want that now lads, would you?'). After the boxers had been allocated their rooms, the team was taken to the Sandymount Boxing Club for training and a weight check. On their return, they were taken in to be fitted with their Olympic outfits and, with no expense spared in a period of austerity, the competitors were soon resplendent in bottle-green blazers and cream flared trousers, together with a selection of fetching polo necks and the best of footwear. Bit by bit, the Olympic experience was beginning to fall into place and on Friday 11 July, the team left the hotel for Collinstown Airport and the trip to Finland.

"The strange thing about the experience in Dublin was that I almost forgot completely about the boxing. I just was in a daze as everything was new and exciting. Firstly, we were given these clothes that were of a quality that I had never seen before, and we looked like film stars walking around the place. We were treated like kings; the food was exceptional, and there was nothing we could have wanted for. Then the morning arrived on which we left, and I was so excited to be flying to London as the experience was just getting better and better."

On the morning of the team's departure, a telegram arrived for John at the hotel reception, and the advice within was to play a pivotal role in how he would perform in the Games. The message had been sent from Belfast, from his trainer Sammy Wallace who had supreme confidence in his protégé. His biggest fear was that he would change the style which had brought him so far. The message read simply: 'Best of luck John, fight your own way'.

In the days before the advent of budget airlines such as easyJet or Ryan Air, the trip to Finland for the Irish team was like the plot of the 1987 film *Planes, Trains and Automobiles* which starred Steve Martin and John Candy. The initial flight to London from Dublin was only the start of a prolonged journey for the athletes. A train then took the Irish contingent across London to Tilbury docks where the overnight ferry to Gothenburg awaited to take them onwards to Sweden. After a prolonged bout of seasickness for the majority of the team, the following morning they duly docked in Gothenburg on the Baltic Sea. However, the team had no time to admire their surroundings, as a further ferry through the Stockholm Archipelago to Turku in Finland was required to get them to within shouting distance of – and a short train ride from – Helsinki.

THE WORLD COMES TO
HELSINKI, 1952

What counts in sport is not the victory,
but the magnificence of the struggle.
– Joe Paterno

The Games of the XV Olympiad, better known as the Helsinki Olympics, were due to commence on 19 July 1952. Finland's capital had originally been selected to host the 1940 Games, however, the outbreak of the Second World War caused their cancellation. Subsequently, the city warded off stiff competition in 1947 to sway the vote of the International Olympic Committee to host the 1952 Games. In doing so, Helsinki with a population of just over 350,000, became the smallest city ever to host a summer Olympics.

Given the fact that the city of Helsinki had almost completed its planning for 1940 Games, the preparations for the 1952 Games were relatively straight-forward. As a consequence, the event was organised to the highest standards, with many observers suggesting that the Games be hosted permanently in Scandinavia. The Finns had completed an original athletes' village for the 1940 Games, however this had been given over for social housing, which necessitated the building of a new facility. Kottby, a town about 10 miles outside Helsinki, was chosen for this purpose and construction of a village for 5,000 athletes commenced. A total of 69 nations sent teams in the Games, an increase of ten on London's total four years previously. Among the countries making their Olympic debuts were the Bahamas, Guatemala, Hong Kong, Indonesia, Israel and Vietnam.

Significantly, after a gap of almost forty years, Russia, in the guise of the Soviet Union, returned to the competition. It soon became apparent that further accommodation would be required, and another village was constructed in Otnäs, which became the home of the Russians – who provided the largest team of 290 athletes – and the other Eastern Bloc athletes. With the Cold War in its infancy, the Russians upped the ante considerably by insisting on having a separate village for their athletes, surrounded by guards and protected by barbed wire. The Helsinki Games were in essence hijacked by the ideological battles of East and West as Russia, together with Hungary, Bulgaria, Romania, Czechoslovakia, Bulgaria and Poland opted to live separately from the Western nations. Their camp was off limits to the other athletes, while pictures of Joseph Stalin adorned the walls in an attempt to inspire the teams. For the scientists and rulers of the Socialist countries, each victory would be triumph for Socialism and the Soviet way of life.

Twelve blocks were constructed in Kottby to house the 61 nations allocated there. Interestingly the Portuguese team – for whatever reason – opted to stay on their ship moored in Helsinki harbour, while the rest of the teams enjoyed the excellent facilities, which included three canteens and, the height of luxury in a shoe-shining service. The Irish competitors were housed in Block 2 along with teams from New Zealand, South Africa, Canada, Holland, Iran and host nation Finland. The biggest shock to the competitors in the village was the proliferation of luxurious hot steam baths – known, of course, as saunas – which after a spot of acclimatisation became a valuable method of controlling weight, especially for the boxers. Indeed the South African contingent became so fond of the Finnish bathing luxury that they conducted their press conferences from the facility, no doubt to the discomfort of the assembled journalists. One of the stranger quirks of the Olympic village was that every window was fitted with a blackout blind, since the Finnish high summer meant that total darkness never fell at night, and it was thought that this might disturb the athletes' precious sleep.

After their short train ride from Helsinki, the Irish team arrived, were assigned their quarters, and soon began to savour the build up to the Games. The biggest initial problem they would face was a fundamental one, namely keeping their weight down. Three separate marquees were erected to cater for the differing tastes of the competitors, with the Irish boxers taking full advantage of the hospitality on offer.

"Finland was so clean and everything was brand new, so it was like luxury for us. The people were friendly and the women were so beautiful that it was just unbelievable. I recall that everything was so relaxed and we were mingling with some of the great stars of sport. Boxing was not even entering into my mind. Coming from post-war Belfast, we thought that the food was a real eye-opener. We went into the tent for a bite to eat on the first day and saw all the biggest steaks, salmon, mountains of potatoes and vegetables, rice, pastas and salads. Best of all it was totally free so, in truth, letting the boxers in among this food was like giving a machine gun to a monkey as it was going to be chaotic."

Sure enough, the feasting came to the attention of the team manager, and one-by-one the boxers were summoned by Christy Murphy who told the well-fed men, in no uncertain terms, to 'lay off the grub!' The boxers went back to watching their weight and knuckled down to the business ahead as training began. On the second day in the village, the Irish boxing team went down to one of the athletes' training tracks to limber up with a bit of light jogging. Manager Christy Murphy left the boxers as he went to tidy up some administration, and the team commenced a gentle workout in the Helsinki sun. After about five laps, each of the members decided to go back to the village. John McNally was determined to undertake some further training, but this time his antics would see him get into Christy Murphy's bad books for the second day running.

"I was feeling great and did about ten circuits of the track, when I thought that I would have a go on the hurdles that had been left on the home straight. Sure enough, I started jumping over the hurdles with some of the sprinters and out of the corner of my eye I could see and then hear Mr Murphy coming across the field to get to me. I knew I was in trouble, but I was young and wanted to keep fit. Let's just say that I got some tongue-lashing for being so silly, but it was an act of stupidity, as I could have fallen and that would have been me out of the Games."

THE GREATEST SHOW
ON EARTH

*We swear that we will take part in the Olympic Games in fair
competition, respecting the regulations which govern them and with
the desire to participate in the true spirit of sportsmanship for the
honour of our country and for the glory of sport.*
– Olympic Oath (1952)

The Olympic Stadium in Helsinki had waited a long time to
claim its place among the great sporting arenas of the world.
Construction on the massive arena, which lies two miles outside
the centre of Helsinki in the Töölö district, had begun in February
1934 and was completed with two years to spare in June 1938, in
preparation for the 1940 Games. However, history intervened and
the onset of the Second World War saw the stadium empty and
lifeless during July 1940. Fate however came to the rescue in 1947,
when the International Olympic Committee presented Helsinki
and the 70,000-capacity stadium with a second chance of glory by
awarding Finland the 1952 Games.

After a quick lick of paint and a dusting down, the
Olympiastadion was ready for action and looking resplendent as
the Games drew near. The opening ceremony for the Helsinki
Olympics was scheduled for the stadium for Saturday 19 July, but
any hopes that the organisers held for good weather were dashed

from early morning. What had been planned as the highlight of the Games was ruined, as steady drizzle and heavy rain alternated with thunder and lightning throughout the day. Despite the downpour, a capacity crowd including the great and the good of world sport and political leaders gathered in the stadium.

The Irish team – very much at home in the weather – were up early as the protocols and rules were read out to them by team manager Christy Murphy. Blazers were brushed clean, shoes were polished to perfection and hair was styled immaculately with Brylcreem, as the time drew near to depart for the stadium. In all, 5,000 athletes representing 69 nations were simultaneously going through the same processes as the military operation to get them to the stadium swung into action. At last, the Irish team was ready: officials with clipboards rapped the doors of the apartments to tell them that the time had come. A gleaming Tricolour of brilliant green, white and orange was placed outside the door – as the athletes emerged to get on their buses, a sense of pride and nerves took hold.

"Basically we had been clicking our heels for a few days, waiting on things to start, but the enthusiasm was still there. Eventually, the day arrived for the opening ceremony and the first thing we all noticed was that the weather was atrocious. But this was just like the weather back home, so we just got on with it. The whole ceremony took four hours and we were soaked right though. Our blazers, shirts and trousers, shoes and socks were sodden and it quickly turned into a farce as the rain got heavier and heavier."

The ceremonies began with the customary Parade of Nations, led according to tradition by the Greek team. The other teams followed in alphabetical order and the host team was the last to enter the Stadium. Squeezed in between Iran and Italy came Ireland, but after enduring the worst of the Finnish summer for two hours in the field adjacent to the stadium, all the athletes wanted to do was get the ceremony over, and go back to their quarters. Traditionally, the host nation tries to outdo the previous hosts in putting on a more spectacular show, and despite the weather Finland pulled out all the stops.

The highlight of the day came when the Olympic flame entered the stadium in the hand of Paavo Nurmi, the legendary long distance runner who was featured on the official poster for the Games. The athletes broke ranks to catch a glimpse of Nurmi who lit the cauldron on the field. Four children then carried the torch to the top of the Stadium tower where the official flame was lit by the sixty-three-year-old Finn, Hannes Kolehmainen, long distance runner and holder of four Olympic gold medals. There was a disruption in the proceedings when German peace activist Barbara Rotbraut-Pleyer gained access to the track and ran to the speaker's rostrum in order to deliver her message for world peace. She was immediately dubbed the 'Peace Angel' by the assembled press. The gymnast Heikki Savolainen, medallist at four previous Olympic Games, swore the Olympic oath on behalf of the athletes:

"We swear that we will take part in the Olympic Games in fair competition, respecting the regulations which govern them and with the desire to participate in the true spirit of sportsmanship for the honour of our country and for the glory of sport."

Eventually, after further pomp and circumstance, including the release of 6,000 doves, the President of Finland, Mr Juho Kusti Paasikivi declared the Games open. With steam rising from their soaking backs, the Irish team left the stadium and returned to their quarters for a well-deserved shower and a chance to relax. However, one of the boxers was to regret his haste.

"To say that we were soaked to the skin was an understatement," recalled John McNally. *"We got on the bus and the windows were steamed up, and we just felt miserable in the cold and rain. All we*

wanted was a shower, and the new-fangled shower units in the village were something that we had never seen back home. In those days if you wanted a shower in any of the boxing clubs you had to make do with cold water from a pump, as that was the only choice you had. Kevin Martin the lightweight was first back, and he turned on the shower and came out to get undressed. When he went in, we heard the most terrible screams, as he had jumped underneath scalding water and burnt his back. He was in a bad way and we had to call for a doctor to attend to him, as he was coming out in blisters – he really was in agony and shock."

After treatment, Kevin Martin was deemed fit to box in the Games, but his back held the evidence of his rashness. Boxing was not due to commence until Monday 28 July, which gave the pugilists a full week to prepare for their first bouts. The team took full advantage of free access to the events at the Olympic Stadium, and kept themselves fit as their moments of truth drew near.

THE TIME FOR TALKING
IS OVER

The essential thing in life is not conquering, but fighting well.
— Pierre de Coubertin

Of the 69 competing countries at the Helsinki Olympics, 44 sent teams of boxers. In all, a record 240 fighters, which included for the first-time representatives from Russia and Bulgaria, entered the ten weight divisions. Unlike in previous Games, boxers who reached the finals were awarded either gold or silver medals, while the beaten semi-finalists were given a diploma of achievement and a bronze medal. Previously, a box-off was required to determine third place. This departure was welcomed by the competitors in that no 'box-off' for a bronze was staged. The argument that the sport of boxing had been diminished by awarding two bronze medals was soon lost and medals continue to be awarded to both beaten semi-finalists.

The Irish boxing team was allocated exclusive use of one of the boxing gyms for a period of one hour each day. The Irish fighters were given the lunchtime slot between the Americans and the Canadians, and McNally and company met up with and became acquainted with future stars such as Floyd Patterson and Chuck Adkins in the changing areas. Whilst John McNally revelled in the experience, he also studied the Americans intensely, watching out for one man who would be favourite to take gold, and the man out for revenge over McNally: Mr Jake Corvino of the United States.

"I had fought Corvino in the Stadium and he was a tough cookie. I was certain that he would be at the Olympics, and he would be out to reverse the decision I got over him. So, I casually struck up a conversation with the American coach Pete Milo, and asked him where Jake was. He looked at me and gave a look of disgust as he replied:

'Don't talk to me about Jake Corvino! That guy only toured with the Golden Gloves so that he could see his grandmother in Italy. All the women in Manhattan are dying about him, and he has no interest in boxing if you ask me. Anyway Jake La Motta says he wants to sign him up as a professional – we are better off without him, son.' That gave me a lift as I was expecting him to be there, and I didn't fancy meeting him to be truthful."

Milo became friendly with McNally and began to take an interest in his progress. One afternoon, the American coach stayed behind to watch the Irish team work out, and he was soon mesmerised as the main event of the routine took place: the sparring between John McNally and Terry Milligan. Whilst both Belfastmen were great friends and had been sparring partners for a long time, when they entered the ring all friendships were set aside for the duration. Milligan, especially, was a total advocate of the belief that sparring was something which should be done at the fastest possible pace, bordering on all-out combat.

McNally agreed with this philosophy and was game for Milligan, otherwise it was a total farce. Americans, Canadians and officials stopped to stare as the exchanges began between the two friends. Jabs, hooks and uppercuts were exchanged with lightning efficiency and accuracy as the exhibition gathered momentum. As the rounds progressed, no quarter was given and no prisoners taken as the spectators were treated to a fantastic display of speed, accuracy and agility. By the end, both boys were exhausted. As they

Maisie McNally – John's Mother who died in 1945.
"For months I heard my Father cry himself to sleep at night."

John McNally's pictured in 1939 wearing his first
communion outfit.

Left to right: Jimmy Bannon, Rose McNally, George McNally Sr,
and John pictured in 1945.

John (left) sparring as a Juvenile in 1948 with
clubmate Jackie Mitchell.

John with his trainer Sammy Wallace – In the early days the White
City Club had no gym and training took place in Wallace's back yard.

John after beating Richard Jenkins, ABA Champion,
Ulster Hall, 1951.

John working out with Sammy Wallace in 1951. The sign on the wall
says 'No Fees, No Training' – times were tough!

The loyal supporters: John's father George Senior,
brother George Jr, and Sammy Wallace.

Above and right: John represents Ireland in a bout against Jake
Carvino (New York Golden Gloves Champion) in April 1952.
"I thought that the stadium was about to come down round me"
remembers John.

IRISH AMATEUR BOXING ASSOCIATION

Corinthian Boxing Club present

GRAND TOURNAMENT

at

NATIONAL STADIUM

on

FRIDAY, 6th JUNE, 1952

GREEN CORNER   *YELLOW CORNER*

5 STONE SCHOOLBOY CONTEST—3 x 1½ Minute Rounds.
1. J. O'NEILL (Cors.)   v.   P. BYRNE (Transport)

9 STONE YOUTH CONTEST—3 x 2 Minute Rounds.
2. P. McCARTHY (Cors.)   v.   P. DEANS (Sandymount)

FEATHERWEIGHT CONTEST—4 x 2 Minute Rounds.
3. T. BUTLER (Cors.)   v.   P. MARTIN (St. Vincent's)

LIGHTWEIGHT CONTEST—4 x 2 Minute Rounds.
4. M. McCULLAGH (Cors.)   v.   J. SWEENEY (Avona)

LIGHTWELTER CONTEST—4 x 2 Minute Rounds.
5. W. REDDY (Cors.)   v.   G. ARNOLD (Avona)

HEAVYWEIGHT CONTEST—4 x 2 Minute Rounds.
6. T. BRUCE (Sandymount)   v.   J. NISCO (D.U.)

OLYMPIC TRIALS

BANTAMWEIGHT CONTEST—3 x 3 Minute Rounds.
7. P. KELTY (Cors.)   v.   J. McNALLY (Belfast)

LIGHTWEIGHT CONTEST—3 x 3 Minute Rounds.
8. K. MARTIN (Mount Street)   v.   A. BYRNE (Drogheda)

FLYWEIGHT CONTEST—4 x 2 Minute Rounds.
9. A. REDDY (Sandymount)   v.   CPL. W. O'BRIEN (Portobello)

FEATHERWEIGHT CONTEST—4 x 2 Minute Rounds.
10. T. LYNAM (Cors.)   v.   J. BYRNE (Mullingar)

WELTERWEIGHT CONTEST—4 x 2 Minute Rounds.
11. E. McKEON (Cors.)   v.   J. McLOUGHLIN (Sandymount)

CRUISERWEIGHT CONTEST—4 x 2 Minute Rounds.
12. T. CLANCY (St. Vincent's)   v.   R. GANNON (Parnells)

HEAVYWEIGHT CONTEST—4 x 2 Minute Rounds.
13. D. MAHER   v.   GNR. C. CAROON
(British Railways)   (4th Field Artillery, Mullingar)

PROGRAMME   :   :   **2d.**

ARDIFF

Programme from 6 June 1952. His victory over Kelty saw John
finally qualify for the Olympics.

Terry Milligan, Harry Perry and John McNally pictured before an international against Scotland at Dublin's National Stadium in 1952.

The Irish Olympic squad on the boat to Helsinki.
John is in the back row on the second left.

The opening Helsinki Olympics ceremony. Distance runner Paavo Nurmi carries the torch around the rain-soaked stadium.

An overhead view of the Olympic Stadium.

The Olympic Village – "The food was so good we thought we'd died and gone to Heaven."

Welterweight
'The Ironman' Peter Crotty

Lightweight
Kevin Martin

Light Heavyweight
Willie Duggan

Flyweight
Ando Reddy

The Irish Olympic Boxers pictured in Helsinki.

Boxers in the sun in Helsinki, on the left is Olympic wrestler, Jackie Vard.

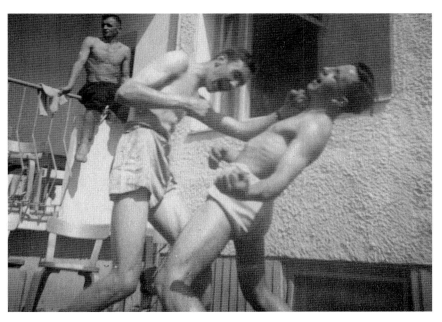

John McNally and Ando Reddy indulge in mock sparring.

Boxers and officials pictured in Helsinki.

Official team photograph. John is second from left, front row.

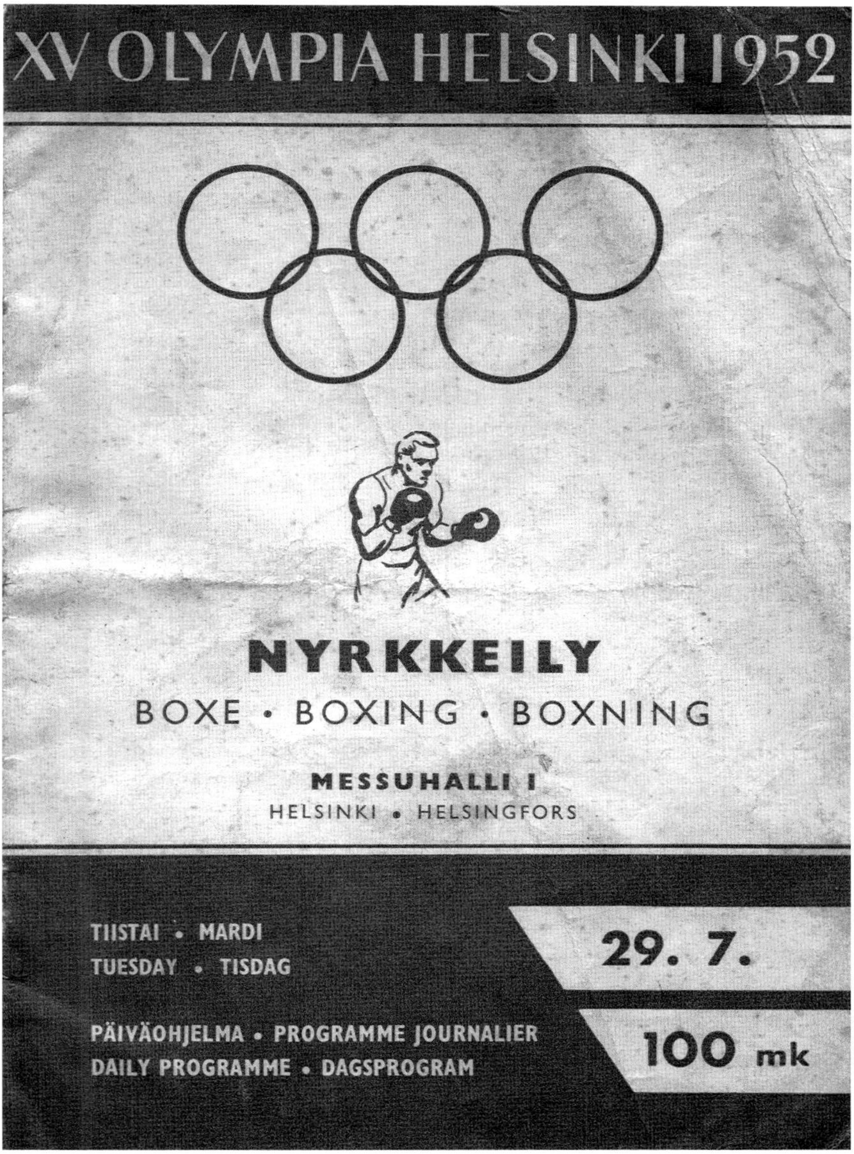

Boxing programme from the Helsinki Olympics.

John's Olympic Medal.

shook hands and warmed down, the word was spreading from the gymnasium that Ireland had two fighters (McNally and Milligan) who were ready to make their mark in the boxing arena.

"Terry and I just went for each other as there was no point in taking it easy, given what lay ahead. This caught the eye of the Americans and the Canadians, and they thought we were crazy for giving it our all. When they heard that Terry and I were the best of friends they just couldn't take it in."

On the Wednesday morning prior to the commencement of the boxing on Saturday, all the boxers were required to report to the arena – the massive Messuhalli (Exhibition Hall) – for the obligatory weigh-in. Each of the competitors lined up in their respective weight divisions, while the formalities took place. As he waited in the queue, John was to witness something that has stayed with him ever since – a display of arrogance that was met with an act of defiant and perfect courtesy.

"There was an Egyptian boxer called Ibrahaim Abdrabbou standing in front of me," he recalled. *"I was chatting as best I could to him when I noticed that this Iranian competitor by the name of Nickhah was turning round and giving him some abuse. The Egyptian stood 6ft, which, for a bantamweight, was amazing, and the Iranian was suggesting that he would knock him over in a fight. There was also some very nasty abuse shouted down the line by the Iranian, as Abdrabbou's face was getting redder and redder all the time. Eventually, I suggested to him that he should respond, as there was no way that he could stand there and take such abuse – indeed I offered to back him up. What he said to me just shook me to the core as I have never met a man so humble and without malice."*

What the Egyptian said in response was perfect, in the true spirit of the Olympic ideal. Abdrabbou, whilst being on the end of some very nasty insults from the Iranian, turned to John McNally and said:

"Irishman, I did not rise to the bait, for I will do my talking in the ring. Always remember this my friend: when somebody has beaten you, take your hat off to them; and when you beat somebody, take your hat off to them also – but make sure it fits your head when you put it back on."

The entire Irish contingent weighed in under their respective weights and it was a case of now waiting for the draw to be made. Just after lunchtime on Wednesday, Christy Murphy arrived back at the village with the news all the boxers had been waiting for. With a cigarette in one hand and a piece of paper in the other, he began:

"So, here's the way it is boys. Ando Reddy, you've got the Italian Pozzali. John McNally, you got a 'bye' into the next round. Tommy Reddy, you will fight a guy from Yugoslavia called Redli. Kevin Martin, a Belgian called Van de Keere. Terry Milligan, someone from Iran called Afsharpour. Peter Crotty, the Swede Gunnarsson. Willie Duggan, Tita from Romania and John Lyttle, some French guy called Lansiaux."

John McNally had touched lucky, as fortune had given him direct entry into the second round. However, for the rest of the Irish team it was a case of preparing for competition, which would commence two days later on 28 July. First of the Irish into the arena would be Dubliner Andrew 'Ando' Reddy against the Italian southpaw and hot favourite Aristide Pozzali, who had taken gold in the flyweight division at the 1951 European Championships in Milan. Although he fought gamely, Reddy was duly outclassed by Pozzali who dominated the fight and came away with a unanimous decision. Pozzali's performance put him in pole position in the division, but he was to lose in the next round to the Russian Anatoli Bulakov, who was himself beaten in the semi-final by the eventual silver medallist, Germany's Edgar Basel. However, Reddy's performance did not bode well for the Irish team, and it was indeed a poor start.

That evening, Ando's brother Tommy entered the ring in the featherweight division where the Yugoslav Stevan Redli awaited. It was to be another bad experience for the Irish, as Tommy became the second of the team to be eliminated. He had no answer to the power of Redli, and the referee was forced to stop the bout in the second round. Redli was in turn eliminated in the following round when Leonard Leisching of South Africa won on a unanimous decision. It was clear that the Olympic Games were proving to be a severe test of the Irish boxers who had been used to parochial boxing within the country. The Irish boxing squad urgently needed a boost.

That boost came from the hands of Kevin Martin in the lightweight division. He had won his place in Helsinki the hard way, having seen off the undoubted class of Tony Byrne, Dave Connell and John Cummins to get the nod for the lightweight berth. Martin was an Olympic veteran who had reached the second round in the featherweight class four years previously in London. He lost on points to the Italian Ernesto Formenti who went on to claim the gold medal. Therefore, it was evident that Martin had the pedigree as he faced up to Belgium's Marcel Van de Keere. Using his experience, though perhaps hindered by his injury in the scalding shower, Martin came away with a split decision to register Ireland's first victory: the prospect of a whitewash was averted.

At middleweight, it was now the turn of Terry Milligan, arguably the best (certainly the most exciting) of all homespun amateur champions to take to the main stage. Milligan had laid down a marker at the 1951 European Games in Milan, when he took a bronze medal in the light-welterweight class. At those championships, Ireland claimed two further medals when John Kelly won silver at bantamweight, while Dave Connell took a bronze in the featherweight class. Standing in Milligan's way was the relatively unknown Iranian Ebrahim Afsharpour. John McNally watched with interest as Milligan entered the ring, since his performance would provide a clue as to how he himself was shaping up. As it turned out, Milligan gave an exemplary display of skilled boxing. He was fit, sharp and supremely accurate as he coasted to a unanimous decision. In the arena, Milligan's sparring partner took note of his friend's assured display and grew in confidence as his first bout drew near. As the first day of competition drew to a close, it was 'two out, two still in' for Ireland.

Tuesday morning saw the Irish contingent return to the arena in defiant mood. First into battle was the Dungarvan-born Army representative Peter Crotty. The 'Iron Man' as he was known was a truly outstanding international for Ireland throughout the 1940s and early 1950s. Boxing out of the St Mary's Club in Clonmel, Crotty was untouchable in his native country and in 1952 he captured his fourth successive Irish title at welterweight. He possessed a fierce punch, was fast on his feet and had represented Europe in the Golden Gloves Championships in Chicago in 1951. By the end of his career, he would notch up 74 appearances for Ireland. He had the ability to go far in the Games and his opening opponent was the unfancied Swede, Harry Gunnarsson.

Fate intervened in the bout and left Crotty distraught and out, as a clash of heads finished his Olympic Games. The Waterford man was cruising in his bout and had won the first two rounds by proverbial miles. In the third, the boxers got into a clinch and a crack of heads was audible from the ringside. The net result was that Crotty sustained a serious cut above his eye, which immediately came to the referee's attention. From that moment on, Crotty was on borrowed time and fighting for his survival. The battle was lost though as blood streamed into his eye and the referee was forced to stop the contest. Crotty was led to his corner, and he lost on the cruellest of twists of Fate. Ironically, the following day, Gunnarsson was unable to fulfil his second round fixture against Vescovi of Italy due to the pummelling that Crotty had given him. However, the sad demise of Crotty touched everyone in the Irish camp, and luck was most definitely deserting the boxers.

Willie Duggan's performance at middleweight did little to raise morale in the camp. His bout against the Romanian champion Vasili Tita was neck-and-neck as the fight entered the second round. Duggan then had a proverbial rush of blood to the head, and landed the cleanest of blows on his opponent's forehead. The only problem was that the Duggan delivered the blow with his own forehead, right in front of the referee's eyes. Since he had been warned previously about this deviation from Queensberry Rules, the referee was left with no option but to disqualify the Irishman. Duggan had broken the eleventh commandment in boxing: 'Don't get caught!' Tita was to storm through the middleweight division and claim the silver medal. However, he was stopped in the first round of the final by future legend Floyd Patterson.

At heavyweight, it was now John Lyttle's turn to restore some pride. After he had given the American Ed Saunders a battle royal in Dublin that April, much was expected. His bout with the Frenchman Jean Lansiaux was a tough and uncompromising affair. The two boxers went at each other from the off, and after three rounds Lansiaux was awarded the narrowest of split decisions. For Ireland, it was now a case of 'five down, two through' with John McNally ready to make his entrance.

"REMEMBER, IF YOU HEAR A BELL, KEEP GOING!"

Boxing is for men, and is about men and is men. A celebration of the
lost religion of masculinity all the more trenchant
for being lost.
— Joyce Carol Oates

John McNally's Olympic Games began in earnest on 30 July 1952. The previous day, 14 of the 23 entrants in the bantamweight class had fought it out for the right to reach the second round, joining the 9 boxers – including McNally – who had been afforded byes. Standing in the opposite corner from the Belfastman that Wednesday morning was the champion of the Philippines, Alejandro Ortuoste, who had also been afforded a bye in the opening round. With the Irish team down to three survivors, the pressure was on McNally to perform and prove his credentials as a worthy Olympian. All the trials and tribulations which he had gone through to get to Helsinki were now at the forefront of his mind, and he was aware that his detractors back in Ireland were watching his progress with great interest. As he approached the ring in his crisp green vest, coach Christy Murphy issued John with some very sound advice:

"Remember John there are two rings in operation at once in here. One has a buzzer and one has a bell. If you hear a bell, keep going. Stop

71

and you will get your block knocked off. Only stop when you hear the buzzer, I will say it again – the buzzer, as that, and only that, means that it is the end of the round. Nothing else, you hear?"

John McNally was well aware of this pitfall, having observed the opening contests and, indeed, grimaced as some of the fighters were caught clean after mistaking the bell for the buzzer, and vice versa. His thoughts were on the task ahead, and staying out of the reach of his opponent. The rest of the Irish team and a majority of the Americans were in attendance at ringside, for the anticipation had grown that McNally was about to explode onto the scene and show that he had the skill and courage to go far in the Games.

"I wasn't nervous to the extent that I thought I would be, and was glad to finally be getting into action. For some reason, I just became very calm as I entered the ring and concentrated on the task in hand. Jackie Vard, the Irish wrestler at the Games, ended up in the corner along with Frank Cooper and they gave just a slap on the face and said to go for it, and I did."

Piston-like left hands rained down on Ortuoste during the opening three minutes. McNally's speed and footwork made him a difficult target, and he built up a decisive lead with swift jabs and uppercuts that landed with predictable regularity. At the end of the round, little advice was needed in McNally's corner as he had gained the upper hand. Cooper's mantra to all the boxers was simple: 'deep breaths, chin down, and left hand out'. Taking his advice from the telegram sent to him by Sammy Wallace, John fought his own fight, and went on to impress the assembled crowd as he quickened the pace and controlled the bout until its ultimate conclusion; a unanimous points victory.

The fact was that, in hindsight, Alejandro Ortuoste was no pushover. He went on to take the bantamweight gold medal at the Asian Games in 1954 and his defeat to McNally was seen as a major upset in the Filipino camp. However, it was a case of 'job done', and the Irish bantamweight became the third representative to progress. Described in the *Belfast Telegraph* as a 'grand display', McNally's confidence soared, as he had overcome the first step and proved that he was capable. The only question was – how far could he go?

That night, back at the Irish team's apartment, the defeated boxers moved out of their rooms and were given the smallest rooms. The three survivors, McNally, Martin and Milligan were placed together in the biggest room in the apartment. This was to allow them space and privacy as the climax of the Games drew near. By Saturday morning, the day of the finals, only one bed would be left occupied.

Lightweight Kevin Martin was still smarting from his scalding in the showers, but his mind was focused totally on his next opponent, Gheorghe Fiat from Romania. Fiat had 'motored' his way past the Egyptian, Mohyi Eldin Elhamaky, in his opening bout and the contest with Martin was considered to be too close to call. Despite his experience, Martin was overwhelmed by Fiat and found it difficult to deal with his all-out attacking. Just as in London four years previously, Martin lost his second round bout by a unanimous decision. He was down, devastated and out. The hopes of the Irish team now rested on the two Belfast boxers, Milligan and McNally.

In the light-welterweight division, Terry Milligan was on fire. His first round victory had seen him at his best in the perfect arena. In his second contest, he was drawn against Dutchman Pieter van Klaveren, who had come through a hard encounter against Canada's Roy Keenan in his first bout. Van Klaveren's family had some pedigree when it came to Olympic boxing. His elder brother Lambertus 'Bep' van Klaveren – known as the Dutch Windmill – had taken a gold medal in the featherweight division at the 1928 Games which were held in Amsterdam. It would be a significant scalp for Milligan if he could record a victory over van Klaveren. With a quarter-final spot at place, Milligan showed the form that he was capable of and gave the Dutchman the run-around for the full nine minutes of the bout. He was never troubled throughout, and became the first of the Belfast contingent to get within touching distance of a medal by gaining a unanimous verdict. It was now up to McNally to follow suit.

If the Filipino Ortuoste was somewhat of an unknown quantity, Vincenzo Dall'osso had a reputation second-to-none. In 1951 in Milan, the Italian had beaten Ireland's John Kelly in the final of the European Championships to claim gold in the bantamweight class. The Italian was considered to be the hottest of favourites, as his name was drawn against the novice McNally in the quarter-final. In his previous contest, Dall'osso had seen off the humble Egyptian Ibrahaim Abdrabbou – who most likely took his hat off to the Italian – by unanimous decision and had set his eyes on the Olympic title.

"I was just so confident that I didn't care who I was meeting in the quarter-final," said John McNally. *"Ever since I had beaten Jake Corvino in the National Stadium in April, I felt that I could face anyone. I was fit, I was right mentally and I knew I was fast – very fast."*

The fight took place of Thursday 31 July, and with the final scheduled for the following Saturday the pressure was most definitely telling. Dall'osso was short and stocky, and tried to work inside the taller McNally as the bout commenced. The Irishman's long left jab kept the bobbing Italian at bay for most of the round, but on the occasions on which Dall'osso did get inside he scored with tattoos of lefts. In the second round, the Italian employed rushing tactics, which allowed McNally to move and score from distance. Whilst Dall'osso chased and harried McNally, the Irishman picked off his opponent continually with his straight left and the result was never in doubt. Again, the judges were swayed by McNally's composure and speed and gave him a unanimous decision. The semi-final awaited the ever-confident Belfast boxer. McNally and Milligan were the last two athletes remaining in the 'elite room' at the Irish apartment.

Just as John McNally had seen off the threat of an Italian European champion in his quarter-final, Terry Milligan would face a similar test in the light-welterweight division. In 1951, Bruno Visintin had swept through the lightweight class at the European Championships in Milan to claim gold. In his opening contest at Helsinki, Visintin knocked out Ernesto Porto of the Philippines in the second round, while Juan Curet Alvarez of Puerto Rico – a future USA amateur champion – had been easily dispatched on points in his previous outing. The nineteen-year-old Italian was skilful, but seasoned observers felt that Milligan would have enough craft and astuteness to beat him. This proved not to be the case for Milligan, and he was out-boxed and outfoxed by the young Italian who progressed to the semi-final. In that semi-final, the Italian met his match, in the form of America's Chuck Adkins, the eventual gold medallist. The final of the light-welterweight division saw the first boxing clash between the United States and the Soviet Union, when Adkins defeated Viktor Mednov in the final by a 2-1 split decision.

John McNally was now the last Irishman standing and had the 'elite' bedroom all to himself. As Friday dawned, the whole of the Irish party fell in behind John McNally in his quest for glory. Nine minutes separated the Belfast boxer from becoming the first Irishman to win his way to an Olympic boxing final. However, the nineteen-year-old had maintained his inner belief and was still supremely confident as the bout approached.

"The pressure most definitely did begin to weigh down on me after Terry was eliminated," remembered John. *"It helped though that he had such a good temperament and didn't get down about the whole*

thing. Terry was very philosophical about life, and just accepted the defeat."

The semi-final draw would see McNally go toe-to-toe with the tough Kang Joon-Ho from South Korea. In his opening bout, the Korean had defeated the Iranian Nickhah — whom it seems had overestimated his own capabilities while boasting to Egyptian Ibrahaim Abdrabbou at the weigh-in for the Games. Kang had emerged as a serious contender after he had seen off the American David Moore by a split decision in his quarter-final. Moore was to turn professional on his return to the States, where he was known as the Little Giant. Standing just 5ft 2in, Moore won the world featherweight crown in 1959 when he defeated the legendary Hogan Bassey. After five defences of his crown, Moore was to die tragically after a bout with the Cuban boxer Ultiminio 'Sugar' Ramos in 1963. In the tenth round of their bout, Moore was knocked down, damaging his brain stem in the fall. Moore collapsed and died a week later. His death ignited a debate on the future of boxing in the United States. Such was the impact of his death that Bob Dylan recorded a tribute to the boxer entitled 'Who Killed Davey Moore'.

In the early part of his semi-final contest, McNally had to deal with some clever attacking from the Korean, but gradually he began to assert himself and, with some clever defensive boxing, soon took command. At the mid-point of the second round, McNally unleashed a vicious onslaught that floored Kang: thereafter the outcome was clear. He continued his onslaught and punished Kang in the third round with some vicious combinations.

"I remember hitting Kang in the third round and he winced," said John. *"I looked over at the referee, as the Korean had taken so much punishment at that stage that it was a foregone conclusion that I would win."*

The moment of truth arrived after nine minutes and, as expected, McNally was the unanimous winner. He stood now on the threshold of history the following day, and was installed as favourite for the title. Back in Ireland, the word spread that a young boxer from Belfast was into the Olympic final. The radio and newspapers were full of praise for the fresh-faced youth, and his star was rising. Despite the victory, McNally had no time to wallow in the glory. Two medics accosted him outside the ring to take a look at his back, which had been shredded by the ropes during the contest. Immediately, they sent him to the dressing room to have the wounds dressed. John remembers the event:

"Once there, a medic took out a bottle of pure alcohol and told me to lie face down on a bench, and warned me that the alcohol would sting my back badly. I recall there were two boxers lying meditating on the benches beside me, preparing mentally for their bouts. Both got up immediately and took one of my hands each in preparation for the treatment. To this day, I can feel the pain, and still smell the alcohol on my back. It was terrible and I was about to scream so I squeezed the boxers' hands so hard in a reaction to the pain. Only later did I come to realise that the men who held my hands that day were Floyd Patterson and Charles Adkins – two legends in the making. It is an act of kindness that I have never forgotten."

That night in the Messuhalli, officials oversaw the removal of the extra ring in the arena. The finals were a complete sell-out and a majority of the crowd were hoping that the darling of Finnish boxing, Pentti Hämäläinen, could beat John McNally and claim the gold medal on the last day of competitive action. Irish team manager Frank Cooper took John into Helsinki to relax that evening, and there they took in the Humphrey Bogart classic *The African Queen* – dubbed in Finnish, subtitled in English.

Later, John McNally slept soundly, undisturbed in the Irish quarters. He and many in Ireland awoke the following morning with the anticipation of a gold medal being won in Helsinki on Saturday 2 August 1952.

BAD DAY AT THE MESSUHALLI

"Whether 'tis nobler in the mind to suffer
The slings and arrows of outrageous fortune"
from *Hamlet*, William Shakespeare

In 1992 Michael Carruth's victory in the welterweight final at the Barcelona Olympic Games was witnessed live by a vast section of Ireland's population, who had risen early for the event. Live satellite coverage was by then the norm, whilst communications in the intervening period have reached levels that people in 1992 could scarcely have imagined. The Helsinki Olympic Games of 1952 were usually reported in newspapers back home the day after events occurred, and dispatches were at best sketchy. No live television or radio coverage was provided back in Ireland or Britain – RTÉ television did not start broadcasting until 1961 – and many relied on local cinemas to provide newsreel footage of the Games, many days after the event had taken place. On the evening that John McNally stepped into the ring for the final, cinemas back in Ireland were probably showing footage of the opening ceremony two weeks previously. However, the quickest method of finding out the result of the final came courtesy of the *Belfast Telegraph* in Royal Avenue. In that era, the *Telegraph* had above its entrance a rolling news screen which displayed in lights the latest news from the 'wires' as

79

and when it was received. On the Saturday evening of John's final, the street was packed with family, friends and well-wishers awaiting news from the screen. In Dublin, the crowds had also gathered by the 'wires' in anticipation of a victory, whilst in Helsinki the Irishman of the moment was going through his paces.

In hindsight, from the opening bell of the bantamweight class, Pentti Olavi Hämäläinen of Finland and John McNally of Ireland were destined to meet in the final. Both boxers had been the best in the bantamweight division by a mile. The bottom line was though that the final would either give Ireland its first-ever gold medal at boxing, or the host nation would be rejoicing in glory. Pentti was the undredog, but the odds were stacking against John McNally.

Pentti Hämäläinen was born on 19 December 1929, in Kotka, Finland. He took up boxing at an early age and in no time was considered to be the best amateur prospect in Scandinavia. In 1951 along with Ireland's Peter Crotty, the Finn had represented Europe against the American Golden Gloves Champions, and later that year took home a bronze medal from the European Championships in Milan in the flyweight class. Add to this the fact that he was boxing in his home country, in front of a partisan crowd: it was clear that the Finn was going to be a tough man to beat.

Hämäläinen went into the final with an immaculate record of four wins at the Games, all by unanimous verdict. Great Britain's Tommy Nicholls – who would take silver at featherweight in Melbourne in 1956, beating Hämäläinen in the process – posed few questions of the Finn in their 1952 opening bout. A similar fate awaited Poland's Henryk Niedzwiedzki, who would claim bronze at Melbourne; he could not deal with Pentti's style of all-action aggression. In the quarter-final, South African Helmuth von Gravenitz succumbed without much fuss to the Finn, and the home nation began to sense that a gold medal was a distinct possibility.

Russia's Gennadij Garbuzov stood between Pentti and the final: their fight was one of the highlights of the tournament. This bout was, according to most pundits, the hardest duel seen in the arena. Despite the fact that Hämäläinen continually caught the Russian square on the jaw, he refused to back off and kept coming at the Finn. The arena was on its feet at the final bell, and appreciation turned to ecstasy as the hometown favourite received the unanimous vote of the judges. Speaking to the press after watching Pentti, McNally told them that he was impressed, but felt that he was in with a good chance of taking the title. As usual, in defiant tone, John added that his opponent was 'fast with a good punch, but I'll be ready for him'.

The highlight of the finals' night was indeed the clash of McNally and Hämäläinen. The hall was packed with partisan Finns eager to witness history being made at the expense of the Irishman: the atmosphere, at times, reached fever pitch. First into the ring that evening was the flyweight decider between Nathan Brooks of the United States and the West German representative Edgar Basel. Brooks was a truly outstanding amateur, winning the Chicago Golden Gloves titles in 1950 and 1951. In the Olympic final, he comprehensively outpointed Basel to take the title with a unanimous decision.

As the formalities of the presentation ceremony were being observed, McNally and his seconds were pacing the dressing room awaiting the signal to emerge into the arena. Eventually, the official arrived and there was no turning back. The arena remained indifferent as the green vest made its way to the ring, but erupted in cheers as the figure of Hämäläinen in his blue vest was glimpsed entering the hall.

The bell signalled the beginning of the most important nine minutes of each boxer's career. The opening exchanges were tentative as McNally used his left lead to keep the crouching southpaw at bay. Pentti scored well with a number of lefts and rights which had the Irishman on the retreat. The first round had been too close to call. In the second, McNally opened up and caught the Finn with a combination which had him on the ropes, where he scored with some neat right hands. Each time Pentti attacked, the noise in the arena rose to thunderous levels, whilst every blow landed – whether accurate or not – was greeted with raucous uproar. For all his rushing tactics, McNally was weathering the Finn's attacks and using his counter-punching style to land his own clean blows. As John McNally recalled, it was a messy fight throughout, but he felt that he had done enough.

"Pentti was cautioned at least eight times during the bout for hitting with the inside of the glove and for using his head to open my eye, which in today's rules would have lost him points. At the end of each round, I asked my corner why the crowd were on their feet, as his blows were not landing on me."

When the final bell sounded, the crowd stood expectantly, and the boxers embraced in the centre of the ring. Within two minutes, the decision would be known and greeted by either emphatic approval or discontented derision. The fighters went to their opposite corners to exchange pleasantries and retired to await their fate. Each of the three judges checked and rechecked their card, and eventually the officials handed the result to the master of ceremonies. The boxers stood in the middle of the arena, where brilliant light illuminated the spectacle. All eyes were concentrated on three men, one wearing a green vest, one a blue vest and the referee in a crisp clean white shirt. For John McNally, all went into slow motion as the seemingly endless announcements began. The small Irish contingent of Olympians and officials were living on their nerves. It came down to another trio: Mr Mason the British judge gave it to Ireland; Mr Schwinger, the American, gave it to the Finn, while Austrian judge Mr Stascha gave the decisive vote to Hämäläinen.

End of story. McNally loses. That, as they say, is that.

As expected, the decision was greeted with emphatic and prolonged approval in the hall. Tough medicine for the Irishman.

"He got it on a split decision and I could not believe when his hand was raised: it was like a nightmare come true. I was devastated and in floods of tears because I was convinced that I had won the gold medal. I was so low that I still find it hard to think back on those few minutes, as it really was a hard blow to take after coming so far. The fact was that, regardless of how I felt, I had no time to compose myself, as everything was working like clockwork and I had to carry on with the formalities. Immediately after the fight, they held the medal ceremony in the ring, but I was so cut up about the whole thing that it was all a blur. My silver medal was no consolation, and the fact that the crowd were in raptures only made me even more depressed."

The *Daily Telegraph*'s reporter at ringside, Lainson Wood, described the result as 'the last fling of outrageous fortune of the 1952 Olympic Games'. He added that the decision had 'cast its poisoned arrow in the direction of Britain when John McNally from Belfast was beaten in the final of the bantamweight contest'. Despite the correspondent's apparent oversight regarding the fact that McNally was representing Ireland, his view was shared by most of the Western media in attendance. Lainson continued:

> 'Hämäläinen, a strong and courageous little Finn, was permitted, without caution, by one of the worst referees of this ill-assorted band, to land swinging punches with his forearms and the heel of his glove. McNally weathered the tempestuous attacks assailing him like the good boxer he is and cut and bruised the Finn with smart counter blows. He won every round according to British reckoning.'

In addition, Wood contended that McNally's counter-punching had provided the cutting edge and the judges had exercised their partiality by awarding the fight to the Eastern European country, as Finland was considered to be.

McNally kept his composure during the medal ceremony and watched as the Irish flag was hoisted for the first time in an Olympic boxing arena – below the flag of Finland. Only later did the Irish contingent learn that the 'anthem' lined up on the turntable by officials, should McNally have won, was 'It's a Long Way to Tipperary'. Perhaps, for John, it was just not meant to be. Back in Belfast, Dublin, Cork and Limerick, the rolling news displayed in lights the simple message *'McNally loses Olympic Final...more soon'*. The people shrugged their shoulders and drifted home, unaware of the drama that had taken place in Helsinki. *The Official Report of the Organising Committee for the Games of the XV Olympiad Helsinki 1952*, as produced by the IOC, made special reference to the clash between the Irishman and the Finn. While it referred to the partisan atmosphere in the arena, it had the Finn as the sure winner.

> 'The bantamweight final between the Finn Pentti Hämäläinen and the Irishman John McNally raised enthusiasm in the Hall to a climax. Hämäläinen, the shorter of the two, attacked indefatigably, giving the Irishman, who favoured long-range boxing, no opportunity for an exchange of punches on equal terms.'

Meanwhile, the official report prepared by the Irish Olympic Council carried a quote from Christy Murphy about the bout:

> 'Most independent persons considered that the referee failed to make any effort to enforce the rules of boxing against the Finn, who was naturally anxious to win and who knew he had little chance at orthodox boxing against a stylist of McNally's calibre.'

A losing dressing room after an Olympic final is truly a depressing place. Muhammad Ali once pointed out that 'nobody knows what to say in a loser's locker room'. The silence of defeat is truly deafening. The shattering of a dream – especially in disputed circumstances – can be a hard station for a nineteen-year-old to comprehend. The sounds of prolonged cheering travelled the short distance from the arena as Pentti made his way from the ring. The Irish dressing room was in silence as many solemn well-wishers tried their best to console the vanquished silver medallist. All John wanted at that stage was to get out of the arena, out of Helsinki, and home to the Pound Loney to be comforted by his family.

"Sure, it could be worse John," said Christy Murphy. But inside McNally's mind, he was truly shattered by the experience he had just been through. Since the beginning of 1952, the bantamweight had passed all the tests which had been placed before him. Irish junior and senior stars, seasoned internationals, Golden Gloves and European champions, together with classy Olympians, had all succumbed to McNally's speed and strength. Regardless, the manner in which McNally had been toppled was painful, and a sore lesson in sporting politics. Eventually, Pentti Hämäläinen made his way into the Irish dressing room, and the two boxers talked about the fight. John still felt aggrieved and told the Finn that he felt the decision was wrong. In a generous gesture, Pentti offered to come to Dublin so as a rematch could take place on Irish soil. No Olympic medal would be at stake – just pride – but the two boxers shook on the deal and the rematch was on.

Despondency did not take long to evaporate, as John and the Irish team returned to the village and took stock of the silver medal win. That evening, Olympic officials were out in force advising the respective teams of the arrangements for the closing ceremony, which would take place the following day. Thankfully, the gods were kinder with the weather that Sunday and, to the relief of the athletes, the ceremony was a much simpler occasion than the opening one. As Ireland's only medallist, John McNally was given the honour of carrying the Irish flag and leading the team around the Stadium. The Olympic flame was extinguished as the official fanfare reverberated around the Stadium, and the Olympic flag was lowered as an orchestra and choir performed the hymn of the Helsinki Games. The flags of the participating nations followed the Olympic flag out of the Stadium, and the Finnish national anthem brought ceremonies to a close. It was over. Finished. Gone. A fantastic experience for the Irish team was ending. From the heights of Helsinki, three ferries, two trains and one plane would bring them home to Ireland and mundane everyday life.

THE HISTORY MAN
RETURNS A HERO

In the future everyone will be famous for fifteen minutes.
– Andy Warhol

The Irish summer of 1952 was a total washout, yet in those days nobody blamed the concept of 'Global Warming'. It was just accepted as the way of life. The Irish Olympians arrived in Collinstown Airport outside Dublin on the morning of Friday 8 August, to a less-than-rapturous reception. There, among the families and good friends waiting for the heroes, were John's proud father George, and his trainer from the White City Club, Sammy Wallace, who both threw their arms around their hero. John's medal – a thing of beauty at 95% pure silver – was proudly produced and received many admiring glances from those present, but there was nobody as proud as the three Belfastmen. George McNally wanted to do his son proud, and told John that he had arranged for the trio to stay over in Dublin until Saturday, as there was "some business" he needed to attend to in the capital.

That particular business was getting on the phone to Belfast to ensure that the arrangements were in place for the silver medallist's arrival at the Great Northern Railway station in Great Victoria Street, at 1.00 pm the following afternoon. Outside the airport's arrivals hall, a single representative from Irish radio was enquiring as to where he could find John McNally. Eventually, he found McNally and conducted a two-minute interview, an edited version of which was broadcast on the news at ten o'clock that night. In the interview, John again said that he had been 'cut up' by the decision, but added that there was no point in looking back as it was now history.

Dublin's weather that Saturday morning was wet and miserable, as the McNallys – Sammy Wallace had gone on ahead – boarded the Northern train. In the Belfast-published *Irish News* that day an article on the front page entitled 'Big Reception Planned for Belfast Olympic Medal Winner' advised readers that a parade from the train station would commence at 1.30 pm. It would proceed through the centre of Belfast, up to the White City Club, and back to John's house at 13 Cinnamond Street. The omens were bad, however, as the steady rain began to get heavier. By midday the weather had become torrential. As the train headed through Drogheda, Dundalk, Newry and Portadown the silver medallist was blissfully unaware of the reception that lay in store.

By 1.00 pm the Belfast train station was thronged with many thousands of well-wishers, undeterred by the incessant downpour. As the steam train approached, the crowd rushed the barrier: police were forced to hold them back as the situation began to get out of hand. As McNally left the train, he noticed the multitudes in the distance, but thought that they were on their way to some other event. Then the penny dropped. Thunderous applause and cheering greeted John as he approached the ticket barrier, and he was soon engulfed by well-wishers who hoisted him shoulder-high through the station. Outside, the parish band, St Peter's Brass and Reed, struck up 'When Irish Eyes are Smiling' as John was greeted by chants of 'We want McNally!' Such was the enthusiasm that John was put on to the roof of the taxi which had been waiting to bring him on his journey home. Eventually, after much delay, the parade began, with his club mates from the White City leading the way with a banner reading 'We are proud of you, John'. The taxi and the band followed suit and the crowds got bigger as the procession neared the City Hall. However – just like the opening ceremony of the Olympics – John was totally soaked to the skin, as the Irish weather did its utmost to ruin the occasion. The people of Belfast though were not going to let the rain dampen the event as, for the first time in the city's history, they were now welcoming home an Olympic medal winner.

"I could not believe my eyes when I saw the crowds in Belfast," recalled John. *"When they came through the barriers at the station I thought that I was going to be attacked for some strange reason, such was the chaos. It continued outside the station and the cheers and applause just got louder and louder the further we got. The one thing I will never forget is the weather, as it was atrocious. Everyone was dripping with rain, but the crowds stayed and cheered. They all wanted to see my medal, and I thought that I would lose it in the crush so they put me on top of the taxi and I just held it aloft the whole way."*

The procession snaked its way through the city, up North Queen Street, across the Shankill Road, down to the Falls, into Divis Street. Finally, it entered the Pound Loney. The Pound was decorated with banners and John was mobbed as he walked through the tight streets until he reached Cinnamond Street, which was packed with well-wishers. John thanked the crowds for turning out and said that he was exhausted but so happy to be home. To a reporter from the *Irish News*, he denied rumours that he was about to turn professional and said that he would take a break from boxing but keep in training. After many hugs and slaps on the back, he entered No. 13, where his sisters and brother, George, awaited. After an emotional reunion, John went out the back of the house, scaled the wall, and sneaked over to Crane Street to see his grandmother Rose. He was home. Tired, wet and emotional he was soon to collapse into bed, as excitement waned and the prospect of a return to work that Monday dawned.

That night, the Ritz Cinema on Belfast's Great Victoria Street was hosting the premier of the movie *Jim Thorpe – All American*. Starring Burt Lancaster in the title role, the film told the story of Jim Thorpe, the Native American who had been stripped of his Olympic gold medals after it was discovered he had played for a professional baseball team. The medals were reinstated in 1983; thirty years after his death. The guest of honour that evening in 1952 was John McNally – his proud family were all seated in the private box overlooking the stage. Before John was invited onto the stage to be introduced to the audience, Sammy Wallace approached him to say that a prominent Belfast Unionist dignitary – who was to make a presentation – was insisting that the boxer remove his Ireland blazer, since it had a Irish Tricolour embroidered on its breast pocket.

The history of flags and emblems in Northern Ireland has been fraught, but in 1952 the status of the Irish Tricolour was something that caused consternation in Unionist ranks. Two years later, in 1954, the Stormont Government passed the Flags and Emblems Act which effectively banned the flying of the Republic's flag in the North. However, in the Ritz Cinema that wet night, McNally's blazer was considered offensive by the politician. John took Sammy Wallace's advice and removed his blazer so as to not offend anyone; he has regretted it ever since. It was a poor end to a fabulous day, as politics had impinged on sport. It was a case of 'welcome home to Belfast, John McNally!'

LET THE GOOD TIMES ROLL

"Made it Ma! Top of the world!"
– Cody Jarrett in *White Heat*

In the Falls Road area of Belfast, John McNally was the nearest thing to a superstar since the actor James Mason had been 'shot' and 'fell injured' in Boomer Street during the making of the classic Carol Reed film *Odd Man Out*. Outside of sport, John's star was still on the rise and the postman each morning brought letters from girls across Ireland asking the Olympian to become their pen pal, as well other requests of a more 'romantic' nature. Everywhere he went, people stopped him for a chat and he became a celebrity in his own right. The Catholic Young Men's Society organised a door-to-door collection as a 'thank you' and the parish priest, Father McCloskey, presented John with a wallet containing a crisp £50 note as a token of the district's appreciation. He also had the honour of kicking-off local soccer's Gold Cup Final at Cliftonville's Solitude ground, and was the honorary judge at a number of beauty contests in provincial towns. Many hospitals for sick children were visited, shops opened, young boxers presented with trophies and invites to dinners received in the months after John's return. Things were looking good for the shy lad from the Loney.

August became September as summer turned to autumn and John McNally returned to proper training in the White City Club, where the membership had rocketed since the Helsinki Games. Sammy Wallace put his charge through his paces and found him just as eager and strong as he had been before the Games. The Olympian's only problem was that making the bantamweight limit was becoming a fight in itself. McNally's first bout was scheduled for Thursday 30 October at the Ulster Hall, where he was topping the bill in an exhibition organised by a sergeant in the Royal Ulster Constabulary called Albert Smyth. John recalls:

"Sergeant Smyth was a boxing fanatic and a real gentleman. Shortly after I had returned from Helsinki, I had promised him that I would box in the Ulster Hall on a bill he was trying to put together. The show was an absolute sell-out, and as a reward he told me to go to McMaster's tool shop in Belfast and pick up some work tools, and tell them to send the bill to him. I couldn't let him down."

Touring Ireland that week was the full West German international team. They were scheduled to meet Ireland – with McNally as bantamweight – on Hallowe'en night, twenty-four hours after John's Ulster Hall appointment. Word reached Dublin that McNally was to fight in the Ulster Hall and a telegram was dispatched to Cinnamond Street, expressing the Boxing Association's displeasure and advising McNally that he should forego the Belfast bout. John, however, honoured his promise to Sergeant Smyth, and boxed in the Ulster Hall that night. Whilst he chose to ignore the advice from Dublin, his exploits in the Bedford Street venue lasted all of twenty-nine seconds – including the count – as his English opponent, John Hawthorne, was knocked-out cold. The following evening John entered the National Stadium to indifference from the Irish officials, and prepared for his second outing in twenty-four hours, this time against a German champion.

Prior to the commencement of the bouts, both teams were introduced to the crowd from the ring and each boxer received a warm reception. John McNally's reception was overwhelming, as the crowd stood and applauded the Belfast boy in recognition of his Olympic achievements. Before the anthems, an additional ceremony took place: John was presented with the Boxer of the Year award from Christy Murphy of the Irish Boxing Association. The bantamweight bout saw McNally clash with Eric Schidan, the 1951 West German champion, in a contest that the Belfast fighter controlled throughout. As the *Irish Times* reported the following day, 'McNally had not only a greater range of punishing blows, but he also had the speed of footwork that kept him safe from Schidan's attacks'.

For the record, the international finished level at five bouts each, but things were just getting better and better for John McNally. He was proving that his exploits before, during and now after Helsinki were no flash in the pan and he really was a class act in the ring.

His next competitive bout came in early December in the National Stadium, when he was included in an Irish select squad to box a visiting German Select team. The Crumlin Amateur Boxing Club in Dublin sponsored the event and the Irish squad wore that club's colours in the ring. Although not a full international, the Stadium was filled to capacity by fans eager to see the star McNally on his return. Fritz Rings was the reigning West German bantamweight champion, but had been overlooked for the Olympic Games. A clash with the silver medallist was his chance to prove his point. It was not to be. McNally had Rings on the ropes from the first bell as he treated the crowd to some of the form he had shown in the Olympics. His speed and sharpness left the German on the back foot, and the decision was never in doubt from the off. In the space of five weeks, McNally had taken the scalps of two German bantamweight champions.

Exhibition matches were a weekly occurrence now for John McNally. In mid-December, at the invitation of Colonel Jim Kelly of the Irish Army, he undertook a visit to Cork to fight in the City's Town Hall. Kelly paid the fare not only for John, but also for his brother George, and their father, George Senior, to accompany the star. They all stayed in Cork's top hotel, and a civic reception was hosted by the Mayor of Cork, Patrick McGrath, in honour of the Belfastman. All over the city on the day of the exhibition, posters appeared with the simple message: *'Town Hall Tonight – Boxing – John McNally'*. For an Irish silver medallist in 1952, that was all that was required to pack an arena out. As the year came to an end, John McNally could look back on a fantastic year with thoughts of greater exploits to come in 1953.

THE GOLDEN BOY OF
IRISH SPORT

Even the longest day will have its end.
– Irish Proverb

If 1952 was bad in weather terms, the first month of 1953, did not promise much for the year ahead. Storms lashed the whole of Ireland, while on 31 January disaster struck off the coast of Larne. The *Princess Victoria*, a British Railways car ferry, was making its way from Stranraer in Scotland to the Co. Antrim town during one of the worst storms in living memory. The ship stalled in the high sea, water flooded onto the car deck, and she then toppled into the dark channel and sank within hours. One hundred and thirty-three lives were lost to the sea that night in the tragedy.

In Belfast, John McNally's boxing year began when he became the German bantamweight champion. I kid you not. There is an old saying regarding the No. 73 bus: you wait for ages on one and then three come along once. In John McNally's case, the same could be said of German bantamweight champions. In February 1953 an Ulster Select fought a visiting German Select in the Co. Down town of Newry. McNally was matched with Emile Malek, a former bantamweight champion of West Germany. The Belfastman was again the star of the night and the German had no answer for his speed and strength. At the end of the

95

tournament – which finished in a draw at three bouts each – the President of the German Boxing Association, Mr E. Keubler, made a presentation to John and declared him the honorary German bantamweight champion for 1953. In broken English, he paid tribute to the Irishman for his feat in beating the three top German bantamweights in a period of three and a half months.

After a word in his ear by the President of the Ulster Boxing Council, John McNally chose not to enter that year's Ulster Senior Championships: his two fellow club mates, Davy Bell and Harry Hunter, met in the final. In March, the bantamweight division of the Irish senior class had only two entrants: McNally and fellow Olympian Ando Reddy, who had moved up from flyweight. The final took place on 21 March, and was a messy affair throughout. Reddy fought hard to get inside the champion, but McNally was considered to be a clear winner on the night, with the speed of his hands the telling factor. That was, unless you were two of the three judges at ringside. In front of a partisan Dublin crowd, Reddy was awarded the decision and the jinx of Helsinki had come home to roost in Ireland. Shortly after the fight, trainer Sammy Wallace was told that John was required to report to the office – Christy Carroll and other officials of the Association wanted to see him. They wished to apologise in person for the decision that had been given against McNally.

"I went into the office and Mr Carroll offered me his hand and said that he wished to apologise on behalf of the Association for the decision, but there was nothing he could do. He then told me that I had been chosen to box for Ireland against Scotland the following week in both Glasgow and Edinburgh, and then in the European Championships in Warsaw the following month. I felt better, knowing that I had been beaten that night by internal politics that kept the Dubliners well-pleased."

McNally travelled to the Kelvin Hall the following week and duly won his contest against the Scot John Smillie. Jim Murie suffered

Boxing programme from 1953. John's opponent was John Smillie who he beat on points unanimously.

Some of the boys seeing John off on the way to Warsaw. Gerard Burns on the left and family friend Jimmy Crowley on the right.

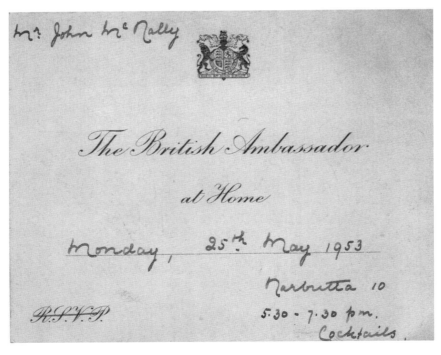

Mr John McNally

The British Ambassador

at Home

Monday, 25th May 1953

Narbutta 10

R.S.V.P.

5.30 - 7.30 pm.

Cocktails

Invitation from the British Ambassador to John during his visit to Warsaw. It was one of the few opportunities he got to relax during the visit.

John pictured in a distinctive pose in Warsaw, 1953.

The European Golden Gloves team arrives in Chicago.

Publicity shot of the team in Chicago. John is in the front row (second left) and his fellow Irishman Terry Milligan is on the far right in the front row.

Ready for action, Union Station, Chicago.

The European Golden Gloves team pose for more publicity shots in Chicago. For a bantamweight, John was almost the tallest member of the team.

American showmanship in Chicago
– The Toddlin' Town.

"All that Jazz" – The tour continues in St Louis.

John and Terry Milligan take time out to pose for
publicity shots at St Louis Zoo.

John during his successful bout for Europe against St Louis Golden
Gloves Champion Andy Gasporovic in St Louis in June 1953.

Meeting local stage stars in St Louis.

Another presentation evening for John McNally, 1953.

defeat at the hands of McNally in Edinburgh later that week and the Olympian was back to his best. However, John McNally's experience in Warsaw in the European Championships was almost to end his boxing career for good.

In May 1953, Warsaw hosted the 10th European Championships, a bi-annual competition that by this stage had turned into a battle of ideologies between East and West. As John McNally matured physically, his problems keeping under the bantamweight limit became very acute, and this was to impact greatly on him in Warsaw. Joining him on the trip to the Communist Bloc was John's trainer Sammy Wallace and old friend Terry Milligan, while Colm Gallagher T.D. and Christy Murphy were the Irish officials. John recalls the visit:

"I remember Poland and Warsaw as a truly depressing place. There were security guards everywhere and soldiers were watching our every move. Even the interpreter we had was changed, as the officials felt that he was getting too friendly with the Irish team. We couldn't leave the hotel without a pass and had to be accompanied everywhere we went by an official."

McNally found himself in a battle to keep his weight down. On the morning of the weigh-in, after fasting for three days, John found himself 2lb over the bantamweight limit. Six heavy rounds of sparring with Terry Milligan, followed by six hard rounds on the pads finally worked up a serious sweat, and then a full hour was the spent in a steam bath: finally John stepped on the scales again. Despite the pleading of Christy Murphy to move up to featherweight, McNally was determined to make the bantamweight, and at 9.58 that morning with two minutes to spare, he weighed in 1 ounce under the limit. That was just the beginning of the weight battle.

"I was not right physically, or mentally, for those Championships," recalled John. *"In the Olympics I was confident, as everything was*

under control, but my mind was worrying about weight; I was fasting and maybe I was beginning to burn myself out."

In his opening fight, John faced the seasoned French boxer, Antoine Martin. The bout was too close to call as it entered the third round. In McNally's corner, Wallace knew that his boxer was not the same man who had stormed through the Olympics. He pleaded with John to give it his all in the last three minutes.

"This will make or break you John," said Wallace. *"You have to find the strength to keep those hands going for three full minutes or you're out. If you go for broke, you will tire him out and that is the only way you can beat him."*

McNally took Wallace's advice and gave the last round all that he had. By the end, he had probably taken more out of himself than the Frenchman had, but he got the decision anyhow. Again, the weight issue was not helping. John spent most of his time in hot baths or skipping to keep the weight down, while tea and toast were the only luxuries that passed his lips. The draw in the quarter-final pitted him again against the southpaw Scot John Smillie, who was the reigning ABA champion. In the end, the tough Scot was comprehensively beaten on points by McNally, who displayed some of the form that had eluded him. He had now assured himself of at least a bronze medal, as had Terry Milligan who had powered through his own quarter-final. That was as good as it got for John though, as he was to meet his match in the semi-final – a Russian by the name of Ivan Stepanov.

Prior to the bout, McNally again fasted to make the weight. This practice saps an athlete's strength; add to that the saunas and training, and it was apparent that something was about to give. Stepanov had been solid, if unspectacular, in his opening bouts. While McNally was struggling to establish his credentials in Warsaw, many observers felt that he was due a great performance, and the Russian would be on the end of such a display. The first round saw McNally use his jab to good effect, but he was like a car with no petrol left in the tank. In the second, the inevitable happened: McNally was caught in a frenzied attack by the Russian that left him cold. Several strong punches caught the Irishman and a beautiful right hook sent him to the canvas for the first time in his career. John got up, but was still dazed as the referee administered the first count – he did not hear the second. Stuck in the corner, he was again caught by a barrage of vicious blows, incapable of defending himself. The last punch of the contest sent him to the floor, out of the championships and into the medical observation ward. A.P. McWeeney then of the *Irish Independent* described the sad climax of the fight as thus:

'The right to the chin which sent McNally down was a real finisher. The Irishman never got back his full capabilities before Stepanov battered him to the floor again. In the second knockdown, McNally's arms were hanging helplessly by his sides as he slumped down against the ropes in his corner under the Soviet barrage.'

On the way to the medical centre, László Papp, the Hungarian Olympic champion who had lost his own semi-final, hugged McNally and offered his condolences: "It's okay John 'Irlande', I get beat too." For a full two hours, McNally was confined to bed in a semi-conscious state as the doctors observed him. He was diagnosed as suffering from severe exhaustion, and ordered to take a long break from the sport. However, two days later, after Terry Milligan lost in the light-welterweight final, word reached the two Belfastmen that they had been chosen to represent Europe in America at the Golden Gloves tournament, which would see them box in Chicago, New York and St Louis. Any prospect of John McNally taking a break from boxing was now a very, very long shot.

CHICAGO, CHICAGO, IT'S A TODDLIN' TOWN

Always bear in mind that your own resolution to succeed is more important than any other one thing.
– Abraham Lincoln

The Chicago Golden Gloves tournament is one of the 'classics' of the amateur boxing world. Together, with the New York Golden Gloves – and the associated American Intercity Golden Gloves tournament –winning one of these titles is considered to be among the top accolades in world boxing, as well as being a sure-fire entry into the professional ranks. After boxing the cream of Chicago, the European boxers would fly to St Louis to fight the American Intercity Golden Gloves champions. On 10 June 1953, John McNally and Terry Milligan left a Belfast bedecked throughout its Unionist areas with bunting in honour of the recent coronation of Elizabeth II. From Belfast, the two boxers travelled to Dublin and then to Shannon Airport, where they flew for New York to join the rest of the European team. Milligan and McNally were at the time the nearest thing to superstars Irish boxing had, and a trip to the States was an opportunity to catch the eye of the real 'movers and shakers' of the sport.

In New York, the two were greeted like lost sons by Olympic coach Pete Milo, who told them a few home truths about the event.

"You guys listen to me and listen good," he said. *"There are only two boxers that the people over here want to see and that's the two Irish boys, nobody else counts. They have sold 15,000 tickets up in Chicago for this bill and they wouldn't have got half that if you two guys weren't coming."*

A mixed bag of European champions joined the Irish contingent, including one Finn, one Italian, two Frenchmen and three Germans. The squad travelled by train from New York to Chicago and were met at the city's Grand Union Station by Democratic Mayor Richard Joseph Daley. As first citizen of the 'Windy City' for a total of twenty-one years, Daley was known as the 'last of the big city bosses'. In brilliant sunshine, the boxers were stunned by the extent of the welcome as media, marching bands and thousands of spectators turned out for their arrival. At their hotel, the Europeans were shown to their first-class accommodation and bellboys catered to their every whim. Formal dinner for the boxers was a black-tie event, with the great and the good – and maybe the not-so-good – of Chicago society there in force. Of course, the Irish-American lobby could not get enough of McNally and Milligan: they were treated as returning heroes.

The fifteenth meeting of the Chicago Golden Gloves Champions and Europe took place in the massive indoor arena known as Chicago Stadium on Tuesday 16 June 1953. Located on West Madison Street on the city's west side, two weeks prior to the Golden Gloves fights, 'Jersey' Joe Walcott had been knocked-out by Rocky Marciano in front of a capacity crowd. That evening, a massive crowd of 14,291 spectators paid $5 each to see the competition. The organisers worked hard to lower the temperature in the ring, and eventually they got it down to an almost bearable 90°F (32°C).

With the Cold War underway, America was possessed with patriotic spirit and the spectators were vociferous in the cause of their boxers, with anthems and Star Spangled Banners to the fore. However, the two Irish boxers – McNally and Milligan – were given rapturous applause from the sizeable Irish contingent as they were introduced in the ring. First up for Europe was the Italian flyweight, Giacomo Spano, and he was on the wrong end of a points decision to Joe Willie De Meyer. John McNally was matched with the seventeen-year-old wonder boy from Colorado, Junior Trujillo. The fight saw McNally use his experience to the full, and he kept the plucky American on the end of his jab throughout. The piston-like lefts and rights, which had seen McNally storm through the Olympics, were unleashed in the last round, to appreciation from the Irish contingent. Four weeks earlier, in Warsaw, McNally had been confined to bed with exhaustion as he had collapsed in the ring after being knocked out of the European Championships. As he milked the adulation of his victory in Chicago, things had never looked better. With McNally an easy winner it was, however, disappointment for Terry Milligan who lost to Herb Mickles. The European team lost the match by six bouts to four.

After Chicago, the European team travelled to St Louis on the Mississippi River for the second leg of their tour. St Louis' Golden Gloves Champions were a formidable bunch and the arrival of the visitors was greeted by thousands of spectators, jazz bands and the best in Southern hospitality. Steamboat trips up the Mississippi, visits to the top jazz clubs and dining in the best restaurants were the order of the day. The European team, accustomed to the mundane post-war life back home, must have thought they had died and gone to Heaven. The business end of the proceedings took place in the St Louis Arena on Tuesday 23 June. McNally was again victorious as he impressed against the champion Andy Gasparovic, while Terry Milligan was unlucky to lose on points to Joe Reynolds. The match ended in a draw at five bouts each, but spare a thought for the German heavyweight, Herman Schreibauer, who lasted all of thirty seconds in the ring with a man-mountain called Charles Liston. Charles soon changed his name to 'Sonny', became heavyweight champion of the world and the rest is history.

"I was the only one of the team that won both their bouts in America," said John. *"The organisers presented me with an honorary pair of golden gloves and I had them tied around my neck when we arrived at Shannon Airport three days later. The following week, I fought for Europe against an Irish Select in Dublin, and my fight [was] against Belfast's Jimmy Carson. I remember that things began to go sour for me that night. I was in the ring being awarded my Olympic certificate and the Dublin crowd booed me. They were still wary of me as a Northerner, and had taken Ando Reddy to their hearts after he had beaten me in the Irish final. Afterwards, the jet-lag and tiredness set in, and I decided to go and see my doctor in Belfast when I got home."*

Little did John McNally know that he would never fight in a green vest again. Dr Lenfesty ordered him to take a complete rest from boxing, as he was in danger of burning himself out. In those days, a doctor's word – like a clergyman's – was final: totally and absolutely. McNally rested, resigned himself to it and got on with life. Months went by and while he still worked out, his appetite for the game was waning. That was until an old score came back to haunt him.

LOOK OUT OLD PENTTI'S
BACK IN TOWN

Life being what it is, one dreams of revenge.
– Paul Gauguin

In November 1953, a phone call came through to Isaac Agnew's Belfast office, from a man with a Dublin accent asking to speak to Mr John McNally. This was not an unusual occurrence for the Belfast boxer, but this time it was not a journalist but the honourable Colm Gallagher, T.D. for Dublin North Central, President of Corinthians Boxing Club. When John answered the phone, Gallagher got straight to the point.

"Hello there John. Colm Gallagher here. How are you fixed for the last day of January next?" enquired the T.D.

"I don't know, Mr Gallagher," answered John. *"You know the doctor has told me to take time out. Is it an international?"*

"Well, you could say that, but I'll be truthful and tell you what I have in mind," explained Gallagher.

That morning, Gallagher had received a letter via airmail from Finland to advise him that John's old adversary, Pentti Hämäläinen, had accepted an invitation to Dublin to undertake his promised rematch with the silver medallist. The Finn would travel with his

105

brother, Väino and three other boxers, on the understanding that the Corinthians club would cover their expenses for the duration of their stay. The only problem was that Gallagher would need to fill the National Stadium to break even, and 'McNally against Pentti' was a sure-fire winner. Only problem was that John McNally was taking a 'break' from boxing.

The arm-twisting began as the prospect of retribution in the Stadium seemed a very attractive proposition. McNally felt well in himself, as the rest had done him a world of good – the only problem was that the bantamweight limit would prove very difficult to meet. John discussed the prospect of the fight at length with his father and Sammy Wallace, and eventually he agreed to meet Pentti in a fight that would put paid, finally, to any question over the result of the Olympic final. He had eight weeks to prepare and get himself up to peak form.

"I was only fooling myself if I thought that I could have been able to take the Finn that night," said John. *"Dr Lenfesty had told me in July that I was 'burning out', and the only way that I could get the strength and appetite back was to take a full break for at least six months. My good friend Sammy Cosgrove begged me not to take the fight, and I had always held his opinion in the highest esteem. Maybe it was pride, or probably just plain stupidity on my behalf to ignore the medical advice, but when you are twenty-one you think you can beat the world."*

John trained hard in preparation for the bout. Local hero John Kelly was brought in to spar: he was preparing to fight for the European professional bantamweight title against Robert Cohen. Try as he may though, McNally could not shift the weight that had hindered his ambition to stay under the bantamweight limit. Meanwhile, in Dublin, (luckily for Gallagher) the Irish boxing crowd were enticed by the prospect of the rematch and the arena was sold out many weeks before the bout.

The Finns travelled to Dublin by aeroplane for the eagerly anticipated bill, which had been organised under the auspices of the Corinthians Club.

Also lined up on the bill were bouts for Paddy Kelty and Dave Connell, who would meet with the Finns Risto Luukkonen and Pentti Rantiapion respectively, while Terry Milligan was matched with Milding Rostrom. The Finns arrived at Collinstown Airport and were housed in Cathal Brugha Barracks, from where they also trained. The prospect of the clash of what the *Irish Times* termed 'the world's two most outstanding bantamweights' captured the Dublin public's imagination, and the National Stadium was again filled to capacity. Since the Helsinki Games, Pentti had taken part in the 1953 European Championships but failed to recapture his previous form. The problem though was that John McNally was only a shadow of the man that had stormed through to take silver at Helsinki. On the eve of the bout, the local journalists built the fight up to a crescendo, with talk of a McNally victory high on the agenda. A.P. McWeeney in the *Irish Times* was sure that the Belfast boxer would reverse the decision.

'McNally was considered by many competent boxers to have won the Olympic Final…he was a tremendous loser and the cleverer boxer," he said. McWeeney added that: "McNally should be in perfect condition…and should make the pace early on. If he can get that left working he should reverse the decision from Helsinki.'

Ominously, he pointed out that Pentti was a strong boxer and, surprisingly, McNally had not taken a warm-up bout prior to the clash of champions.

On the morning of the fight, both boxers weighed in at the Stadium – the Finn was spot-on the bantamweight limit. However, McNally was 3lb over and this posed a threat to the actual bout. It was unfair on the Finn that his opponent came in over the agreed weight, and the fight was on the verge of being cancelled, only for Gallagher to broker a deal – with a lot of apologising to Pentti. McNally was not ready, neither in mind nor in body.

The following day, the papers reported the predictable result. McNally had lost on a unanimous decision and the Finn had proved his point. The first round saw honours shared, but the bundle of muscle and energy that was Pentti threw caution to the wind when he sensed that he was not facing the same man he encountered in Helsinki. McNally was not allowed to come forward as he was subjected to an 'incessant attack'. The aggression of the Finn had the crowd gasping, as their hero was on the back foot and powerless to deal with the attacks. It was a dejected McNally that had to take the decision full-on and see the champion vindicated, but he knew the spark was not there.

In a further twist of the knife, McWeeney in the *Irish Times* noted that the Olympic champion was 'hardly a world-class boxer, but fully warranted the unanimous decision'. If that was a fair comment on Pentti, what did this say of McNally's performance? The bottom line was that John was not fit – mentally or physically. He was a shadow of the boxer he had been eighteen months previously. His perfection of attitude, fitness and positive thinking was deserting him, as his mind was in turmoil. Later, as the Stadium emptied that cold night, many in the crowd scratched their knowledgeable heads: many more felt short-changed by McNally's performance.

Thereafter, John McNally was to endure a serious crisis of confidence. When you are young and good, you fear nothing. However, when the bubble bursts – as it most definitely did – you are affected and unable to cope since you have not the experience to come through. John McNally moved up a division to featherweight and fought one bout – a successful contest against the Welsh champion Peter Davies in the Ulster Hall. However, he was still not 'right' and was about to make the biggest mistake of his career – all for the promise of a future crock of gold and £40 in his hand in the meantime, to turn professional.

A ONE-WAY TICKET
TO 'PALOOKAVILLE'

"You don't understand. I coulda had class. I coulda been a contender.
I coulda been somebody..."
– Terry Malloy in *On the Waterfront*

Most seasoned observers of professional boxing would agree that the Golden Age of the sport occurred between the late 1940s and 1950s. In the United States especially, the advent of the television age helped to bring the sport to the widest possible audience. Names such as Sugar Ray Robinson, Rocky Marciano, Kid Gavilan, Jake LaMotta, Gene Fullmer, and Carmen Basilio all attained legendary status on the small screen. Regardless of class, colour or creed, a paid boxer could be a means to a lucrative end for many – if managed properly. However, with big money at stake, it was inevitable that the sport would be open to corruption and, in many cases, farce became the order of the day. Betting scams and fight fixing were rife as fortunes were made and lost, with the man in ring usually the last to get paid. Not all was what it seemed as promoters, bookmakers and assorted hangers-on made their fortunes off the backs of the battlers in the ring.

In 1953 in New York City, the Federal Bureau of Investigation began a public inquiry into the workings of the Mafia. One of the key witnesses called to give evidence by the FBI was former world middleweight champion Jake LaMotta. The sporting world was shocked when LaMotta admitted openly that in 1947, at the request of the Mafia, he had 'thrown a fight' against Billy Fox. By 'taking a dive', LaMotta had helped the criminal underworld make a fortune through placing sure-fire bets on Fox. LaMotta was in turn 'rewarded' when the Mafia used its influence to arrange for him a crack at the world title, which he won. LaMotta claimed that the illicit practice was widespread. However, he was a lone voice in that he openly admitted to taking a 'dive', and paid a heavy price. Boxing's credibility was shaken badly by the bombshell.

Hollywood was also exposing the seedier side of the sport. In 1954, Marlon Brando played the iconic role of a washed-up boxer called Terry Malloy in the classic *On the Waterfront*. In that film, Malloy, whilst ruing the day he took a 'dive' in the ring thereby ruining his promising career, uttered the famous quote: 'I could have been a contender' – a sad lament of many boxers. Another famous line described the very act of throwing a fight as taking a 'one-way ticket to Palookaville', a phrase that boxers and promoters knew all too well. In the 1950s anyone entering a professional game could indeed have been a contender, providing they knew the right people, played along with the odd sham and did what they were told. The bottom line was money – making lots of it, and getting out of the game before it was too late.

Two years after the release of *On the Waterfront*, Humphrey Bogart was to star in his last-ever film *The Harder They Fall*, in which he played a publicist for a promising boxer named Toro Moreno. Unknown to Moreno, his rise through the boxing ranks was being managed skilfully by the Mafia, who were operating a betting scam. Eventually, when the Mafia was ready to bet against Moreno, he was matched with a boxer beyond his class and was to be on the receiving end of a brutal beating. Afterwards, when Bogart finds out about the plot, he tells the corrupt promoter – played by Rod Steiger – how he really felt about the way Moreno had been used and abused:

"That man lies in the hospital with a broken jaw. He took the worst beating I ever saw in my life, and you want me to go back there and tell him that all he gets is a lousy $49 and 7c – for a broken jaw? How much would you take?"

Despite the bad publicity, the popularity of boxing in Britain and Ireland was at an all-time high. Professional fighters were plentiful and a boxer could, if he so desired, fight for money seven nights a week. In addition to the licensed bouts, many bills were organised outside the control of the boxing authorities, and were seen as a lucrative way to make a living. The paid game was seen as a handy way to supplement a working man's wages, which in the 1950s averaged £6 a week. Most towns had their own professional shows, where brute force and shrewdness was considered just as effective as skill and class. In Belfast, the winner of a bout in the Ulster Hall on a Saturday night was lucky to walk away with £17 in his pocket. However, this amount was paltry when one considers that the arenas were jam-packed with spectators. The reality was that the prize money was the amount left over after a manager, trainer and promoter had taken their share – yet only the boxer had the bruises to show for it.

Less than two years after the glory of the Helsinki Olympics, John McNally joined the murky world of professional fighting. In March 1954 he left his amateur career behind, and threw in his lot with joint managers Sammy Docherty and Jimmy Callaghan. McNally's signature was secured on a year-long professional basis for an up-front fee of £40. That fee, together with a promise of at least £15 a fight, was an offer too good to turn down at the time. However, other factors closer to home forced the Olympian to turn to the paid game. Later that year, John was to marry his long-term fiancée Kathleen Murray and move into a small terraced house in Malcolmson Street off the Springfield Road. In addition, his apprenticeship at Isaac Agnew's had come to an end, and he was looking for a permanent job. Necessity is, of course, the mother of invention and when John's long-time trainer Sammy Wallace approached him to say that two men wanted to speak to him about turning professional, he duly agreed to meet them.

The three sat down and discussed their plans. Through a haze of rich cigar smoke, the talk had been of fortune, travel, glory and fame with 'Don't you worry about that, John', and 'We'll look after that for you, son' being the order of the day. Little negotiation was needed, and within hours a contract was signed and £40 handed over. John McNally was now tied to Docherty and Callaghan: the long climb up the slippery slope of professional boxing was just beginning. However, there was no grand plan set for the Olympian, and it was a case of fighting as and when a bout presented itself. McNally was not to be given any special treatment in his quest for paid glory in the featherweight division. In reality, he was just another novice on the bottom rung of the ladder. Professional boxing is a sport that will entice many pugilists with the promise of riches, but it's also a hard sport in which money is the bottom line. John McNally was going to learn that fact the hard way. He was now leaving the relatively clean-cut world of the amateur game, an experience that was to be a shock to the system.

Sammy Wallace, the trainer on whom McNally's amateur success had been built, was sidelined as his protégé's newfound professional status put strains on their relationship. Docherty and Callaghan insisted that their own man would train McNally – Johnny McBride from the Shankill Road was appointed to oversee McNally's progress. This was to be the first of many mistakes.

Within a month, an opponent was found for McNally's first bout, an eight-round contest in Glasgow's Kelvin Hall against a local lad called Johnny Kenny. The bout was part of the undercard. The main fight was between the Frenchman Robert Cohen – who had defeated Belfast's John Kelly for the European bantamweight crown – and Edinburgh's Eddie Carson.

"At that stage, I was getting married and we were completely broke and in dire need of money," said John. "I was fed up with the amateur game and had no appetite for it. The only thing I knew was boxing, and I had to cut my losses and turn professional. From being part of a great bunch of lads in the White City, I was now on my own. I was an outsider all of a sudden and it was a lonely existence. I was twenty-one years of age, but I said that I would stick at it for a couple of years to see if I could make a name for myself. The bottom line was that I had very little choice."

As McNally was introduced to the Glasgow crowd, he was afforded a warm welcome from those present, many of whom had seen him box magnificently in the same arena as an amateur. In the opposite corner stood the stark reality of professional boxing. Johnny Kenny was twenty-four years of age, possessed no amateur record of note, and had fought twelve times as a professional, losing on nine occasions. In the real world, the two boxers would not have shared a ring, but this was the professional game. Olympic silver medallist or not, you can only fight what is put in front of you. The fight lasted four minutes and McNally was an easy victor, but nobody in the Kelvin Hall that night was any wiser regarding McNally's potential.

Across the world, the biggest chart hit of 1954 was 'Rock around the Clock' by Bill Haley and the Comets. Obviously, with this new dancing fad in mind, the boxing correspondent of *The Irish News* 'Left Lead' – Denis O'Hara Sr – reported the following day that that 'Johnny's Right had Kenny Rocking'. The printed piece was as brief as McNally's debut had been, with O'Hara writing that 'the Belfastman made no mistake' as he 'dispatched the journeyman Kenny in two rounds'. However, while it was reported that 'Johnny had done it all so calmly' in stopping the Scot, it was noted that 'Kenny, who was still dazed in the dressing room, had stung McNally at times with sharp right hooks to the body'. Despite this, it was a case of 'job done', courtesy of the trusted right hand, and McNally departed the following morning for the Larne ferry with his fee in his back pocket. Nobody had travelled to Glasgow with him, and nobody was waiting in Larne on his return. Welcome to the lonely reality of professional boxing.

The King's Hall in south Belfast is a truly imposing and vast arena and it was to be the venue for John McNally's second paid outing. Two months after his debut, Dundee's Bobby Boland was next into the ring for McNally. Boland had been a truly cracking amateur, who had turned professional in 1946. By the time he faced the Belfastman, he had a record of forty-seven wins and twenty defeats. Boland had proved his credentials in 1951, when he fought for the British featherweight crown against Glaswegian Peter Keenan, in what was described by pundits as one of the hardest and most bloodthirsty battles of that era. Whilst he may have been past his best by 1954, it was evident that the Scot would pose some questions of McNally in front of a hometown King's Hall crowd. Despite the task ahead, McNally described himself to the media as 'fit' and 'confident' ahead of his Belfast debut.

In the end, the powerfully built Scot lost on points, but he had more than shown his experience throughout the eight-round clash. At times, he exposed McNally's relative inexperience with a display of craft and guile. If amateur boxing was all about honest endeavour, paid fighting was all about cunning. McNally had been caught many times during the bout with neatly executed punches. For his trouble he ended up with cuts, bruises and a sum of £20 in recompense. Still, it was money earned, but there was no doubt that the climb up the rankings was to be a long and slow one. The paid game was littered with washed-up journeymen, many of whom, like Boland, were well capable of putting it up to an ambitious novice. John McNally was in the process of learning this unfortunate reality. By going the distance with Boland, the Belfast star was not winning over the boxing public. McNally's sluggish performance was noted by the pundits. It was becoming clear that professional boxing was no respecter of Olympic medals.

John McNally's financial worries were eased somewhat when he found employment in Belfast's shipyard, but the work was only of a seasonal nature and boxing had to take priority. Despite this, it was five months until he had his next outing. A third bout was arranged in October against Eddie McNally from Portadown – no relation of course. Eddie McNally was a veteran of the local undercards and was never in contention for professional honours. His career was in terminal decline as he came to the King's Hall in search of a badly needed victory. His namesake, John, was primed and ready: his five-month lay-off from the ring had left him keen, but frustrated at the same time. He knew that the Belfast boxing fraternity were expecting him to explode onto the paid scene, and his third fight offered him a major opportunity so to do.

The Portadown McNally was described as a 'ruddy-cheeked powerful puncher who threw jabs as if there was a brick in each glove'. Despite this glowing appraisal, his record was one of complete indifference. In twenty-one bouts, he had lost eleven, drawn two and won eight – though seven by way of knockout. Indeed, an indication of how parochial paid fighting was in those days is given in the fact that the Portadown fighter had boxed fellow Irish professional Jim Fisher on five occasions in the space of three years. Who said that variety was the spice of life?

The Irish News boxing correspondent was predicting an upset in the ring that night, by suggesting that the Portadown man 'with his short-arm blows could upset his Belfast namesake'. He put his prediction down to the fact that the Helsinki Olympian had been out of the ring for five months, which was 'a long lay-off for anyone who hopes to make the championship grade'.

The main attraction on the King's Hall bill that evening was the clash of Derry's Billy Kelly and Roy Ankrah of the Gold Coast (now Ghana) for the Empire featherweight crown. The entrances to the balcony in the spacious Belfast arena had been opened in mid-afternoon to cater for the massive influx of spectators, a majority of whom were travelling from Derry. The Kelly fight was the top featherweight bout of the night, while first into the arena was the rather lower key battle of the local McNallys.

Despite predictions, it was John who did all the running and knocked out his namesake with a powerful right hand to the jaw in the second round of the contest. The following Monday, 'Left Lead' in *The Irish News* was apologetic to John McNally and 'glad to admit' that he was wrong in his prediction. Interestingly the pundit noted that McNally had showed class that was reminiscent of his Helsinki form, but added that it was the Belfastman who pulled off, in his view, the surprise by winning. Things were looking up though, as John had performed with confidence in the right arena in front of a crowd of 10,000 spectators.

Later on in the evening, Billy Kelly claimed the Empire title to the delight of the packed hall. In scenes akin to those when Rinty Monaghan claimed the world title in the same ring in 1949, Kelly led the crowd in a rendition of 'When Irish Eyes are Smiling'. While John McNally was a long way from the iconic status of Kelly, with three wins in three outings, he was progressing in the right direction.

THE GOING GETS
DECIDEDLY TOUGHER

No hero is proof against injury.
– Proverb

In the mid 1950s, a crack at a British title for the Lonsdale Belt was the highest accolade that most Belfast professional fighters could aspire to. South of the border, things were more difficult; to make an impression most fighters had to travel to England, since little or no competition existed in the Republic. A majority of boxers, however, were considered also-rans and any form of title fight was something that just never happened. For the more talented though, the path to such heights as a British title took many years, due to the sheer number of fighters plying their trade. Proving oneself as a contender was an arduous task. Fortune, luck, and a knack of being in the right place at the right time, usually helped.

Consequently, to streamline matters, the British Boxing Board of Control oversaw a number of Area Boards – Northern Ireland being one – which were permitted to organise competitions within their area. To win an Area title was considered a stepping-stone to a chance of a crack at the British title. The Northern Ireland featherweight champion in 1954 had been Billy Kelly, but, by taking the Empire title in October that year, he had to relinquish the local crown. As a result, the Northern Ireland featherweight title lay vacant as John McNally went in search of his fourth opponent.

In one of his weekly opinion pieces in late 1954, 'Left Lead' began speculating as to who the local Board should consider matching for the vacant featherweight crown. Surprisingly, for a hack who questioned McNally's credentials before his previous bout, he was singing John's praises as a worthy contender for the title. The main men in the equation for the Northern Ireland Area Board were Joe Quinn, Joe King, Billy Smith and Jackie Willis. However, in language that bordered almost on a heart-felt appeal, the correspondent pleaded the case for McNally. Of the Board's dilemma in nominating two contenders, he wrote:

> 'The whole business would be made one huge joke if John McNally is passed over. And I hope that the Board don't retort that they would like to see John have more experience as a money-fighter before he is considered for the title. He may only have had three paid outings, but remember that until recently he was considered one of the world's outstanding amateurs, and actually took part in the amateur counterpart of a world title fight.'

Meanwhile, as the procrastination continued, John McNally had to content himself in late November with a contest against Southampton's Ken Lawrence, who had lost only seven of his twenty-five contests. Lawrence was highly rated in England and it was felt that he had the ability to trouble McNally. The Ulster Hall in Belfast's Bedford Street was filled to capacity to witness John's fourth outing: they were not disappointed with McNally's assured points' victory. *The Belfast Telegraph* that Monday was glowing in its praise of the Olympian's performance and its correspondent 'The Timekeeper' felt that he had seen enough talent in John to suggest a title challenge in the near future:

'In this young novice we have a rapidly rising title contender who, if handled properly, will undoubtedly win his spurs.'

The following month at the same venue, McNally followed up with an impressive third round knock-out of Joe King, a boxer who had lost sixteen of his twenty-three paid contests. However, in local terms, King's name had been in the frame for a crack at the featherweight crown. McNally's victory was sending out a message regarding his title ambitions. The victory over King placed pressure on the Board to nominate McNally for the vacant title, but the Board paid heed to the accepted pecking order and nominated Joe Quinn – in his sixteenth fight of 1954 – to box Billy Smith for the Area featherweight title. In the Ulster Hall on 18 December, in a rousing battle, Quinn won the contest when he stopped Smith in the eighth round to become champion. John McNally would have to bide his time.

The new year of 1955 promised much for John McNally, but on 22 January his star began to wane. Again, the King's Hall had to open early to allow the crowds that had gathered from midday into the arena. Derry's Billy Kelly had put his British title on the line against the tough Londoner Sammy McCarthy. While the main featherweight clash had the crowds on their feet, the undercard clash at the same weight failed to capture the imagination of the 12,000 punters present. A seasoned, tough and durable fighter, Sheffield's Denny Dawson came to Belfast and after winning over the crowd, gave John McNally the toughest fight of his paid career. Dawson was no pushover and feared nobody, especially 'upstarts' with Olympic medals. He harried, he spoiled, he frustrated and – most importantly – he scored with ease during the eight rounds. As the final bell sounded, to the collective head scratching of the crowd, McNally was awarded a victory, courtesy of the perhaps less-than-observant referee Billy Duncan. Dawson was a veteran whose best days were behind him, but he had still displayed all the tricks, ring craft and punching power. The verdict was greeted by a chorus of boos and catcalls. McNally may have won the bout in the record books, but he had lost according to the knowledgeable crowd in the Hall that night. Later, Billy Kelly gave full value as he outpointed Sammy McCarthy to retain the British title.

John McNally's victory extended his unbeaten record, but he knew within himself that his paid career was floundering. The pressure, the expectation, the failure to perform; all were playing on McNally's mind, as the added stress of injury came to the fore. The 'spark' was missing, and it was a matter of time until this was to be exposed. In a perfect world, John McNally would have been a well-paid mechanic on a good wage, training hard to qualify for the Melbourne Olympics in 1956. However, this was not a perfect world. This was Belfast in the mid 1950s, and the glory of Helsinki had given way to the stark reality of professional boxing.

THE BITTER TASTE
OF DEFEAT

A man is not finished when he is defeated.
He is finished when he quits.
– Richard Nixon

In boxing, as in any sport, the cardinal rule concerning injuries
– especially to the hands – is to do nothing to exacerbate the
problem. In essence, time, rest, and proper medical attention
are the only healers. However, in the 1950s, the use of pain-
killing injections such as Cortisone was a widespread temporary
solution, to ensure that a man could fight through the pain
barrier. Rather than forego a payday in the ring, injections were
used to block out the pain, but they were no solution. By the age
of twenty-one, the tools of John McNally's trade were in a very
bad way. Years of his trademark heavy hitting had left exposed
ridges on the backs of his hands – essentially crush injuries.
The pain that he endured was excruciating and the prospect
of an easy solution was negligible. Each morning John would
awake to find his hands badly swollen, and no relief could be
found. With the injury worsening, the prognosis was not good
for McNally's prospects. Each punch thrown was painful and
causing further damage. Essentially, he was on borrowed time
in the boxing ring.

One evening in early March 1955, a retired Belfast boxer called at John's door to offer some personal advice on how he could best address the problem with his hands. Rinty Monaghan was a living legend in Belfast, and had taken the world flyweight boxing championship at the King's Hall in 1948. He retired undefeated in 1950 at the end of a sixteen-year professional boxing career. He too had suffered crush injuries with his hands, but had found a novel solution to deal with the problem. He had strengthened his hands through chopping wood on the Belfast Castle Estate. Rinty advised John to buy the biggest axe he could get his hands on, and ask the rector at the local St Matthias' Church if he would let him cut some trees in the church's extensive grounds. John duly purchased the axe and set about the wooded slopes of the Glen Road, but whilst he got some relief, the damage had taken hold at a deeper, psychological level.

Eventually, McNally was to get the nod from the local powers-that-be, and he was nominated for a crack at the Area featherweight title. In the ring, Belfast's Joe Quinn was the man whom McNally had to beat in order to win over the ever-growing band of boxing sceptics in his native city. Quinn held the Northern Ireland Area Featherweight title which, in itself, was of course no guarantee of greatness, but it gave him the kudos in the professional world that McNally lacked. Quinn had spent some time in the United States, and on his return took to the paid game with gusto, having twenty fights in just over a year. His fight with McNally was scheduled for the King's Hall on 26 March. The punters were expecting a close bout that the challenger – it was felt – had the ability to shade. With the Area featherweight crown at stake, the King's Hall eagerly anticipated a clash that would go the full twelve rounds.

The first two rounds saw McNally pin Quinn to the ropes, but fail to land a crucial or telling punch. As he sat on his stool at the end of the third, he recalled that he was feeling confident and would soon have the measure of his opponent.

"For the first time in my career I had my manager Jimmy Callaghan in my corner, and I told him that I felt that I could finish the fight in the third, I felt so good. The hands were fine and there was no pain. The bell rang and I got up, but from there on in I just couldn't catch Quinn."

By the ninth round, Quinn had cottoned on to McNally's weakness and fought him at close quarters, constantly finding his range inside his taller opponent. However, with thirty seconds left of that round, McNally caught his opponent with a vicious combination that floored Quinn beside the ropes. The count began as Quinn struggled to regain his composure. On 'nine', the referee raised his hands over the prostrate boxer and was about to end the fight when the bell sounded, literally saving Quinn. Whatever magic was administered during the break in proceedings proved to be enough to save the shaken Quinn, and he held on for a deserved points' victory. McNally had been beaten for the first time in his professional career, and it was a painful experience. He had been a second away from victory but denied. In the dressing room it was apparent that the fight had taken a lot out of him. His face and body were badly bruised, but his injured hands had received the worst punishment. As he was cut out of his bandages it became apparent that his hands would either require surgery or a long lay off was needed.

On the Monday after the clash with Quinn, *The Irish News* told the sad tale of McNally's demise in stark words. It was a case of 'hats off to Joe Quinn' as the darling of the wet summer of 1952 had again come up short in the paid ranks.

"THERE ARE PERSISTENT RUMOURS ABOUT JOHNNY'S HANDS"

Patience is a poultice for all wounds.
– Proverb

A boxer laid up and injured is no use to anybody. Any well-meant advice regarding surgery or a lay-off went unheeded. Four weeks after his clash with Quinn, McNally was to top the bill at the Ulster Hall. His hands were given a series of pain-killing injections as the doctor's advice was ignored in preparation for a bout against Nye Ankrah from the Gold Coast.

The Ulster Hall in Belfast's Bedford Street is a cavernous arena that has played host to some of the most fraught political meetings in Irish history. In boxing terms, it is a place that has witnessed some classic, bloodthirsty, and skilful encounters over the decades, many of which have gone down in local folklore. Its acoustics are such that even the smallest crowd can create an atmosphere akin to that of a baying mob, and many boxers have been inspired and intimidated by the noise that rolls across the venue. This was John McNally's spiritual home, and it was here that he topped the bill on Saturday 23 April 1955, in an attempt to resurrect his faltering career.

It is a well-known fact that there is nowhere to hide in a boxing arena: given the knowledge of the Belfast boxing fraternity, there was definitely nowhere to hide in the Ulster Hall. For a man gasping for air in the unforgiving world of professional boxing, John McNally definitely had a lot to prove against Nye Ankrah of the Gold Coast.

"The people looking after me were basically making it up as they went along in the professional game," said McNally. *"It was a case of 'fight him, fight him, and then we'll get you a fight against him – if the money's right of course'. Regardless of the money being 'right' for them I was getting seventeen quid. Dr Lenfesty had seen my hands and ordered me to take a complete break, but there were too many people depending on me and perhaps I was just too nice to everyone. For every doctor telling me to stop, there was one telling me to ignore such advice and take another shot of whatever painkiller was on the agenda. I was 'a means to an end', and if I could not fight then I was yesterday's news. I was told that there was only one chance and I had to take it – damaged hands or not."*

The early rounds of the bout saw John in fine form, as he treated the crowd to some of his best boxing, including the left-right combinations that had become his trademark in better days. By the fourth round the fans were bored, shouting for John to show more of a killing instinct and finish the job properly. Inexplicably though, McNally stood off his opponent, who must have thought that Christmas had arrived early in the centre of Belfast. The West African began to crowd in and caught McNally at close-quarters, setting the pace of the fight.

McNally seemed to be a shadow of the man who had last graced that arena as an amateur, and was lucky to swing a points' decision. It was a case of a job badly done, in front of a crowd that knew something was sorely missing. 'Left Lead', *The Irish News* correspondent tried his best to be constructive about McNally's performance by saying that John allowed the African to 'look good' and he needed to deal with the 'inside stuff'. The fact was that

126

John McNally was in dire need of a performance to prove his critics wrong about his boxing ability. In the Crown Bar, Robinson's, Kelly's Cellars and other Belfast hostelries that evening, many patrons arriving from the Ulster Hall counted the bubbles in their pints of porter whilst musing over the great conundrum of the boxing age; 'How is that a man who can win an Olympic silver medal can lose his magic in such a short period?' What was wrong with John McNally? Many more were not asking questions, but rather answering them by saying he was finished.

By this stage, John was working as a fitter in the Harland and Wolff shipyard. The money he earned in the 'Yard' was good for the time, and helped alleviate the hardship of the professional boxing game, which had not provided him with the riches he had been promised. Essentially though, he led a nomadic existence in sporting terms, and visited a range of boxing clubs across the city to train. He found a second home in the Ardoyne Boxing Club, but the paid ranks was proving to be a lonely station. The onus was on the individual to train, prepare and turn up as required for the benefit of the promoter. The camaraderie of Helsinki was now ancient history.

"I never saw my manager from one month to another. You would hear a rumour that somebody was trying to match you with some fighter, but half the time it was just idle talk. Then, after training for what seemed like an eternity, word got through that you were to fight such and such on this date and you had to abide by that. The pay was always the same – £15 – but there was neither rhyme nor reason to it. It was a case of being available to make the weight and the contest. The problem was that you were being traded between men like a horse would be at a market fair, with the spitting on, and slapping of, the hands securing a fight."

Perhaps, a change of venue would signal a change in fortune, as John's next fight was fixed at the end of May in Dublin's Donnybrook Bus Station, where Derry's Billy Kelly was to box for the European title against Ray Famechon of France. McNally's opponent was

Teddy Peckham, holder of the Southern Area Featherweight Championship and a veteran of almost 150 professional bouts. Add to that the fact that Billy Kelly had beaten Peckham only by a points' decision a year previously and it was evident that the Londoner was – in Belfast parlance – no mug! The writing was truly on the wall for McNally as he travelled to Dublin. That morning in *The Irish News*, 'Left Lead', a staunch supporter of the Belfastman, had expressed his grave concern:

> 'To tell you the truth, I'm worried about John McNally, who meets Teddy Peckham over eight rounds. John has been having trouble with his hands in his last few bouts and, frankly, I doubt that he has given the injuries time to heal. I hope I'm wrong, but I think that he would have given a much better account of himself if he had waited a few months, until those strained sinews had been properly rested. Definitely he has the defensive skill to outbox the crafty Peckham, who is perched next to Sammy McCarthy in the ratings. But he has been rather disappointing of late, you must admit.'

The downbeat note struck by 'Left Lead' proved correct concerning the fight. It was all over in the seventh round as Peckham hit McNally with a sweet right hand; McNally hit the canvas, and the dressing room was where he woke up. As John McNally recalled:

"I was doing okay I felt, and thought that I had the measure of him and then in the seventh, bang! over I went and the next thing I recall was wakening up in the corner with a crowd around me, and seeing Peckham in his dressing gown opposite. Getting knocked-out is a bit like coming round after you have had a tooth out – you are just not sure where you're at for a while. It didn't take me long to know the score and I had walked onto a sucker punch. It was a case of 'say goodnight John,' and 'let the crying begin'."

Later in the evening, young 'Spider' Kelly was to lose a close decision for the European title. His opponent, the classy Famechon, had lost to Willie Pep for the world title the previous year, but had agreed to come to Dublin to defend his European crown. When Dutch referee Barend Bergstroem raised Famechon's hand, things turned decidedly nasty in the arena. Reporters, seconds, trainers and boxers all took cover in the ring as the missiles rained down. Promoter Jack Solomons had a bucket of water thrown over him, while the referee received a punch in the face for his efforts. The Kelly supporters were seething with anger, and the Gardaí were called to restore order. Boxing was the loser in a night of shame. It was, however, not the last time that crowd violence was to greet a defeat for Kelly.

TIME TO GO BACK TO BASICS

Even if the hopes you started out with are dashed,
hope has to be maintained.
– Seamus Heaney

The summer of 1955 was a period of deep contemplation for John McNally. The dreams of professional glory were evaporating in double-quick time and the reality of daily life was impinging on him and his growing family. Rent and rates had to be paid, food, clothes and other essentials purchased. However, the money for this was not going to be won in the ring, and the McNally family knew this all too well. With children now part of the equation, boxing was becoming more and more irrelevant in the daily grind to make ends meet.

In reality, McNally was making no progress in the paid ranks, and it was a case of holding his hands up and admitting defeat. However, when the period of pain after the Peckham defeat had abated, the work on the road back to contention had to be faced. It was as if the silver medal won in Helsinki was acting as a lead weight around John's neck and something had to be done to prove his worth. Fighter, trainer and manager all met to analyse what had gone wrong with the amateur star. It was time to draw a line under the past, shelving what remained of the original plans and preparing an alternative. It was agreed that the key to renewing McNally's potency lay in toughening him up through intensified training. Thereafter, it was essential that a number of relatively easy bouts be sought to improve his record – and most importantly, his confidence. It sounded all too easy.

A comeback fight was arranged for Saturday 24 September 1955 in the Ulster Hall. His opponent was Belfast-born Johnny Skelly, who had lost sixteen of his twenty-one bouts. Hardly a class act but still a tough nut to crack. Manager Jimmy Callaghan was pulling no punches in the press, by suggesting that the road back for McNally was going to be a long one. The problem was that John McNally, for all his undoubted boxing skill, had come across some tough and seasoned fighters too early in his paid career. The niceties of the amateur game were not observed in the paid ranks, and this had cost him dearly. In addition to his fancy footwork, neat combinations and clever use of the ring, John McNally had to learn how to fight and fight hard. He needed to be able to deal with maulers, brawlers and clever journeymen who treated him with no respect and played upon his youth. However, McNally had a stubborn determination to succeed, and was keen to prove himself in the packed Ulster Hall. Everyone present knew that McNally was struggling, and any talk of a re-birth that night was again premature for the Belfastman.

McNally won the bout on points, but again there was no spark in the ring. The crouching Skelly bamboozled McNally for most of the bout, as if he knew that the Olympian was suffering a crisis of confidence, as well as not having had undertaken any sparring. Skelly used every ounce of guile and craft to frustrate McNally. John's main weapon was the straight left hand, but this was limited in its scope. Again, he stood off his man and failed to press home any advantage he had in terms of skill. Speaking in the dressing room after the bout, McNally said that he 'felt fine' and did not want to exert himself on his first fight back. However, in the last three rounds, McNally had opened up and floored Skelly three times, but the jury was still out.

The next test was to come at the King's Hall two weeks later when the tough Glaswegian Matt Fulton was to be John's opponent. In preparation, two excellent boxers, Jim Fisher and Jimmy Brown, were brought in as McNally's sparring partners. The regime was intense as they sought to toughen McNally in the ring and force him to adopt a more robust attitude. Nothing was held back as the intensity of the sparring seemed to have its desired effect. 'Left Lead' in *The Irish News* praised John's ability to the heavens:

'As long as he can stand off and box his man, McNally is the last word in brilliance. Unfortunately, most tough characters have a distinct aversion at being bounced on the end of a long straight left.'

For John McNally, the last line was to prove eerily accurate in the bout against Fulton. *The Irish News* on the Monday reported that all six Irishmen on the card had been defeated, with an appraisal of McNally that was brutal in its simplicity:

'I'm afraid we can write off John McNally as a pro prospect. Once again John had his faults shown up – this time by a game but comparatively crude Matt Fulton, the Glasgow featherweight. John decided that he had had enough in the seventh round, turned his back on his opponent and went back to his corner.'

If the defeat was hard to take for McNally, the write-up in the paper added further hurt to the physical injury. John hit rock bottom at the age of twenty-three. The fact was that he had been hit, among other things, with stomach cramps during the fight, which made it impossible for him to continue. He spent that night in the Mater Hospital under observation as his condition worsened. That was the part of the drama that the crowd did not witness – the damage, however, had been done.

"I had just had enough at that stage. I wanted so much to run out of the Ulster Hall and scream in frustration. Things were working against me in so many ways. The hands were playing up and I had a constant battle with my weight. The constant stress to improve was not helping me, and there was an expectation on me. This guy Fulton was a skilled boxer and he stood off and attacked me at will. I couldn't handle it and I began to feel nauseous in the ring. By the seventh, I had to walk away. The looks on the guys in the corner told its own tale. They were disappointed but I was just devastated. As far as I was concerned I was finished with boxing, and when I got home the next day I shut the door on the whole fight game."

SECONDS OUT, ROUND TWO

You never get a second chance to make a first impression.
– Proverb

'The best of times and the worst of times'; that was boxing in the 1950s. Packed halls, televised bouts, glory and despair in the ring, all witnessed by the enthralled masses. Boxing was drama, boxing was passion, and everyone loved the game – or so it seemed. For all its glamour, there was also a seedy underside to the game as it generated its own bad publicity. In essence, boxing was a brutal pursuit that had changed little since the days of bare-knuckled fighting. Serious cuts, bruising, indecisive referees and eventual permanent physical damage were all part of the game. The key to success in the paid ranks was a fighter knowing when to leave the game before irrevocable damage was caused. Unfortunately, many never read between the lines, and carried the obvious scars for the rest of their lives. With increased publicity, the brutality was there for all to see. In the early 1950s there were a number of high-profile deaths in the ring, which created a significant body of opinion that felt the sport should be banned. Belfast was no exception and the councillors of the city voted in August 1956 to hold a special meeting at which the future viability of boxing – and wrestling, surprisingly – at the Council-owned Ulster Hall would be discussed.

In the week prior to the special meeting, the Ulster Hall held its first fights of the season: topping the bill was the rejuvenated John McNally. Almost a full year had elapsed since John walked away in despair from Glaswegian Matt Fulton, and a full reappraisal of his future had taken place. Gone was any pretension that he was a natural featherweight and – more significantly – 'a new broom' had swept away his previous management of Docherty and Callaghan. The new man at the helm was former Belfast boxer Jackie Briers, a fellow shipyard worker from the Shankill Road who had big plans for McNally. John's hands had been given sufficient time to recover. It was time to prove the critics wrong.

Tony Russell of Leeds – a man who had lost fourteen of his eighteen bouts – was, in essence, the cannon fodder that was to launch McNally's career for the second time. Briers, John's new manager, was calling the shots to the media prior to McNally's comeback, by suggesting that the Belfast boxer – now a more natural lightweight – had taken things far too quickly in the early part of his paid career. However, things were now going to be totally different. Briers had written to the Northern Ireland Area Council suggesting that his new man should be an automatic choice for a crack at the vacant local lightweight crown. Not surprisingly, given John's progress as a featherweight, the response was 'wait and see'.

The Council was yet to meet to determine the future of boxing on its property so the season's first bill was allowed to proceed. McNally's reappearance had raised expectations and the spectators turned out in force to see the local hero. On Monday, the local press were reporting McNally's victory. The evening had been a triumph and the roof of the Ulster Hall was in danger of lifting off as the Belfast favourite entered the ring after a break of almost a year. His home crowd cheered him from the dressing room and through the ropes to his return. In reality, McNally's opponent was nowhere near even the status of 'journeyman', and he was only an extra in the pantomime of McNally's return. John showboated throughout the two rounds of the fight and picked-off his punches with ease as the crowd cheered him on. Wicked combinations, flashing brilliance and smooth, stylish boxing was the order of the day. However, four minutes of class was easy against a fighter of Russell's pedigree.

In John's corner, Jackie Briers was overheard telling John to 'take it easy' and to 'ration that right-hand' though more for the benefit of the crowd than McNally in all probability. After a minute of the second round, John took his chance, and over went Russell as if hit by a sniper. Game, set and match to the star of Helsinki. In his corner, only two thoughts occupied Russell's mind; the £20 purse he had been offered and, more importantly, would he make the midnight sailing to Stranraer from Larne? In reality, putting John McNally in the ring against Russell was just plain unfair.

Regardless, John was back in the fight game. The question was – for how long? The following week, Belfast City Council voted to allow boxing and wrestling to continue for the time being at the Ulster Hall. The sport had been given a reprieve and a bout was arranged for McNally at the same venue. Lightweight Tommy Mason on 1 September was, in theory, an easy second return fight for McNally.

It was not to be as Liverpudlian Mason gave John a hell of a contest. Referee Jim McCreanor adjudged Mason to be the winner. His decision incurred the wrath of those present in the Ulster Hall. For a full ten minutes, catcalls and stamping of feet were the order of the day as discontent grew. The journalists in the arena were not so sure that McNally had won the fight though. Mason had floored the Belfast man for a count of eight in the last round, and his attacking style had been crucial in the summing-up. Again, McNally stood accused of not being aggressive enough: afterwards Jackie Briers laid down the gauntlet for a rematch.

"We'll fight him anytime – in his home town, just to prove that John is not scared of him, and bubbling with confidence."

137

The fact was that Mason had no reason to fight McNally, as he had come to Belfast and claimed his scalp. Mason was moving on, while the apparent failure of John McNally's second coming was again the talk of the boxing fraternity.

THE LONG AND
UNRAVELLING ROAD

But I have promises to keep,
And miles to go before I sleep
— Robert Frost

There is nobody in the British Isles who would argue with the assertion that the Irish boxing fraternity are truly a knowledgeable bunch. They followed their local boxers with loyalty and on a Saturday night in February 1956, Derry's favourite son, Billy 'Spider' Kelly, brought a considerable crowd from the Maiden City to see his scrap at the King's Hall against Glasgow's Charlie Hill. John McNally was not considered for that bill, but was in attendance for one of the most shocking episodes ever seen in a boxing arena. The paper-thin line between a 'knowledgeable crowd' and a 'rampaging mob' was evident for all to see that night.

Trouble began after the London referee Tommy Little awarded the British featherweight title to the tough Scot in front of 12,000 bemused spectators. Initially, all was calm as the chants and boos rose to a crescendo. Eventually, a few beer bottles found their way into the ring, followed by the first of a barrage of wooden chairs. The great and the good – including the Lord Mayor of Belfast, Mr R.J.R. Harcourt – were hit by flying missiles, as the rioting intensified. The Master of Ceremonies, Mr James Allen, was felled in the ring when a chair hit him full-on as he attempted to restore calm by leading a rendition of 'When Irish Eyes are Smiling'. Undeterred, Allen brushed himself off and made a second attempt at the song, only to suffer the same fate as a second chair caught him unawares from behind. Order was eventually restored only after a series of baton charges within the Hall by the Royal Ulster Constabulary. However, the King's Hall was a mess and boxing had again been dragged through the gutter. It was a sign of the passion and intensity –sometimes hooliganism – that boxing aroused among the masses.

'A boxing man to his bootstraps', was how Ernie Fossey was described by the London *Times* in his 1993 obituary. The Londoner came to Belfast on 6 October 1956 as John McNally's next opponent in his painful climb up the ratings. Fossey would go on to serve the professional fight game as boxer, trainer, second, manager and promoter for well over half a century. The former coalman was truly a hard man, having learnt his trade as a teenager by trading blows with far bigger opponents in a boxing booth at Barnet Fair. He proved to be a durable character and left the Ulster Hall a happy man, after he tested McNally to the full and was awarded a draw.

Damage limitation was required by 'Team McNally', as again he had been found wanting in the ring. Briers immediately went on the offensive in the press, by letting it be known that he had sent a letter to the Northern Ireland Boxing Council 'urgently requesting' that McNally be afforded a shot at the vacant local lightweight title. The press release smacked of slight desperation, given the poor form shown by McNally.

'Let McNally and Paddy Graham meet for the vacant lightweight title. If John wins, he will waive his six months' grace as champion and that's a promise. He will fight Al Sharpe and any other contender that may be around.'

The harsh truth was that John had one only won one of his three contests as a lightweight and any claim to an automatic shot at the local title was, in reality, premature. The problem was that everybody knew for a fact that McNally was not ready. Assertions by Briers about McNally's prowess were spurious, especially to the boxing authorities. Another problem lay in the fact that John was not a natural lightweight – weighing in 4lb and 5lb under the limit, he found it impossible to put weight on or bulk-up. In the nasty world of paid boxing, a 4lb advantage was something that a boxer could ill-afford to give away.

In late October 1956, world news was being dictated by events in Hungary, where a popular revolt against the Soviet Union was put down brutally by its Red Army. The newspapers in Ireland were filled with stories of cruelty and brutality, and in solidarity Ireland took in a number of refugees from Hungary. Meanwhile, in Belfast, the local council of the British Boxing Board ignored the pleas of Jackie Briers. An Austrian by the name of Kurt Ernest was matched with John in the Ulster Hall on 20 October. The 'Iron Man' – as Kurt was known – came to Belfast with ten defeats under his belt in eighteen outings. McNally was gasping for air in the paid ranks and his bout with the Austrian was a make-or-break fight. A cracking bout took place over eight rounds and all was in the balance as the final bell sounded. Billy Duncan, the blood-spattered referee, walked to McNally and raised his hand in victory. However, the Belfast boxer looked frail and tired; the bout had taken a lot out of him. He did show some battling qualities when under attack from Ernest by not flinching at his onslaught. A last round of all-out attacking left McNally ahead and the crowd roared him home. But it had been a gruelling contest, which a man of McNally's class should have won easily. The 'spark' was just not there.

In the following two months, John recorded two neat wins against relatively inexperienced opponents. At Streatham Ice Rink in London in November, John stopped George Martin, a relative novice with three fights under his belt. At a packed King's Hall in January 1957, he impressed when knocking-out Glasgow's Arthur Donnachie, who was undefeated in ten bouts, in the first round of their contest. McNally was reported to have been at his fiercest in that bout, having floored the Scot three times as he eased to victory. The two successive wins were indeed progress for a stuttering career. McNally, now twenty-four, had a big decision to make about his future. The paid ranks were littered with the battered 'corpses' of journeymen who found out too late that they should have left the game a long time ago. If John McNally was to lose the 'journeyman' tag he was going to have make the physical move away from the insular world of Belfast boxing.

Coinciding with John McNally's difficulties in the paid game, Ireland's top amateur boxers were travelling to the Melbourne Olympic Games. At twenty-three years of age, McNally should have been Ireland's main hope for a medal, however that was not to be, and the mantle of the country's top bantamweight had been taken by a young prospect from north Belfast named Freddie Gilroy. The Irish team of 1956 was littered with excellent pugilists and names such as John Caldwell, Fred Tiedt, Tony 'Socks' Byrne and Harry Perry were to prove their class at the Games. By the last night of competition, on the first day of December, the country had secured four medals, with John Caldwell, Freddie Gilroy and Fred Tiedt all claiming bronze and Dublin's Fred Tiedt the sole Irish representative in the finals.

In essence Tiedt, like McNally four years previously, was the victim of a harsh decision, with one journalist describing it as the only blot on what had been a great boxing tournament. History records that Tiedt was beaten on a split decision, but that result was very hotly disputed. His Romanian opponent, Nicolas Linca, was awarded a 3-2 verdict and immediately there were howls of derision around the arena. The anomaly was that Tiedt had been awarded more points in total than the Romanian, but was denied on the majority verdict. It was reported that the President of the

Irish Olympic Council, Lord Killanan, had been asked by an Olympic official to make his way to the ring at the end of the bout, in the belief that the result had gone in Tiedt's favour. Wisely, not counting his chickens, the noble Lord retained his seat, not wishing to tempt fate. A Romanian referee was heard to say to Lord Killanan that Linca had been well beaten. However, it was Tiedt who took the verdict square on the chin. There was to be gold for Ireland in Melbourne, as Ronnie Delaney raced to victory in the 1500 metres event on the same day as Tiedt's defeat. Interestingly, in the Official Report on the Games, as produced by the International Olympic Committee, the fight between Tiedt and Linca was mentioned specifically in dispatches:

> 'Welterweight. – Probably the most unlucky boxer was Tiedt (Ireland), who lost a close final to Linca (Romania). Tiedt had very hard fights in his division against Walasek (Poland), Lane (USA) and Hogarth (Australia).'

The Irish team was feted on its return, from Shannon Airport, through the Midlands, to the Mansion House in Dublin. The great and the good turned out to greet the team which, however small, had excelled itself on the world stage. The Helsinki achievement of John McNally had been eclipsed. Eclipsed totally.

REALITY BEGINS TO BITE

One's past is what one is. It is the only way by which
people should be judged.
– Oscar Wilde

In the 1950s, the notion of 'political correctness' had not been invented, or even thought about for that matter. So it was that John McNally found himself matched with a black boxer who fought under the name of David 'Darkie' Hughes. A tough character from the Tiger Bay district of Cardiff, Hughes had already beaten a rather tame Paddy Graham, the top lightweight in Belfast at the time, so a victory for McNally would make him the main contender for a crack at the local lightweight crown. The bout was fixed for the Belle Vue arena in Manchester and ended in a disappointing draw. Again, John failed to press home any advantage in the ring, but the trip to Manchester opened up some new avenues regarding earning potential.

The fact was that in the late 1950s, the economy in Ireland – North and South – was in trouble. The traditional heavy industries, in the North especially, were in recession and work was at a premium. Despite Harold McMillan's assertion that the people of Britain 'never had it so good', the feel-good economy had yet to visit the Pound Loney. Ireland was suffering mass-emigration to England and the United States. For John McNally, the need to provide for his family was acute, and neither paid boxing nor working in the shipyard were fulfilling their financial promise. Manchester was a different story. Well-paid jobs were easily obtained and with money scarce back in Belfast, John made enquiries about moving to Lancashire to work. The dream of making a good living in the ring was evaporating fast, and his mind was set on a move at the end of 1957. With three young children, Marion, John and James, all under five years, regular money was essential. Boxing was becoming irrelevant and the realities of life were now taking precedence.

McNally's career continued on its mediocre path throughout 1957. Guy Gracia stopped John in the seventh round of their bout in Motherwell in May. In September, he travelled to Cardiff to face Teddy Best, a skilled boxer with a vicious punch. By the seventh round, the bout was considered to be too close to call until Best floored McNally with a strong right hand. Unfortunately for Best, the punch he unleashed was at least three inches below McNally's waistline and outside the spirit of the Queensberry Rules. Best was duly disqualified and McNally awarded the fight. The organisers took the decision in bad grace and refused to pay McNally his agreed fee. It took many months of arguing before his money arrived through the letterbox – £20 short.

The notion of leaving Belfast was still high on John's mind when he was offered £100 at short notice to travel to Newcastle to take on an up-and-coming fighter called Ebe Mensah. That October night in the St James' Hall, McNally was stopped in the seventh round: John's career was now bordering on the desperate.

However, light was glimpsed at the end of the tunnel, when John was nominated for a crack at the vacant Northern Ireland lightweight crown against the formidable Al Sharpe, who hailed from the Immaculata club. It was make-or-break for McNally, as a win would give him credibility and put him in the reckoning for a British title shot.

The fight was fixed for the King's Hall on 23 November and again Derry's Billy Kelly was topping the bill. On the Thursday prior to the bout, Jackie Briers organised a press conference at the Lodge Boxing Club, where McNally was put through his paces. An exhibition of sparring by McNally was the order of the evening. The media hacks in attendance were impressed by McNally's assured display, and by the day of the fight he was made slight favourite to beat Sharpe. However, Sharpe was a clever fighter, capable of mixing it with the best and, as it turned out, he was to use all his experience and guile to grind McNally down and knock him out in the eighth round. That was the end of the road for John McNally, one of the classiest amateurs ever to have graced an Irish ring. He had been sucked in and spat out by the professional game and was now left with little option but to leave Belfast and search for paid work. The glitter was gone and now it was a case of forgetting about boxing and knuckling down to reality. That reality lay in Manchester.

THE BOXING WILDERNESS

I started my ring career as a terrific hitter; then my hands cracked up and I had to resort to boxing and tricks.
— Gene Tunney

The City of Manchester was similar in many ways to the Belfast that John McNally left behind in early March 1958. Back-to-back red-bricked streets housed a vibrant population and, most importantly, well-paid work was abundant. John moved to a city which was still in mourning after the Munich Air Disaster, an event that robbed Manchester United of, perhaps, its greatest-ever set of players, known as the Busby Babes. John found lodgings in the New Bury Road with Belfast expatriates the Allen family, and began his search for work. With engineering experience gained at Belfast shipyard, it was not long until he found employment in ICI, where the pay and conditions were a world removed for those in Belfast.

On a weekly basis, cash was sent home to Belfast as John worked all the overtime going. Boxing was a long-forgotten pursuit as the attraction of good money without stress paid the bills back home. However, the fight game in Manchester was thriving, and when word got about that an Olympic silver medallist was in town, it was not long before McNally was made an offer to return. The man who made that initial approach was a Mancunian by the name of Stan Skinkiss. The prospect of a few bouts was too tempting and McNally began training again in 1959, with the prospect of another comeback on the horizon.

At Ayresome Park in Middlesbrough, on a freezing February night in 1960, McNally made a further comeback. This time his opponent was a total novice by the name of Maurice Cullen, who would go on to prove himself one of the best boxers ever to come out of the north east of England. He was made of stern stuff and had worked in the coal pit since he was fourteen, and was highly thought of as a potential future champion. He would go on to win the British lightweight title, which he lost to Ken Buchanan in 1968. The scalp of John McNally would give Cullen some credibility in only his fourth fight. It proved to be a tough fight for Cullen, as John showed his cuteness in the ring. Though the decision went, as expected, to the Englishman, John had made good money from the fight and immediately it was dispatched back home to Belfast.

Dave Coventry – a man with nine straight wins – was to be John's opponent in the Manchester Free Trade Hall two months later. It was true to say that McNally was only fulfilling fights on the expectation that he would be on the wrong side of the decision. That was the way it turned out, as Coventry knocked John out after seven indifferent rounds. It was money earned for the Belfast veteran, but a sore price to pay, as any remaining credibility was evaporating. Never had the glory of Helsinki been so far away.

The final throw of the dice for John McNally's boxing career came on 6 March 1961 at the Farrer Street Stadium in Middlesbrough, against a boxer by the name of Johnny Nolan. For the Belfast fighter, now aged twenty-eight, it was a sad end to a career that promised so much. In an ideal world, McNally would have been entering his prime, and title shots would have been part and parcel of his career. Instead, it was to end on a meaningless undercard at a smoke-filled northern hall. The question as to where it had all gone wrong was irrelevant as John stepped into the ring guaranteed £100, win, lose or draw. In the end, John McNally won the fight with a third-round knock-out. It was as if he knew that the game was up, and threw caution to the wind. Twenty-four-year-old Nolan succumbed to the old McNally right hand in the third, and over he went, to be counted out in what was to be the last fight of his career.

For John McNally it was 'game over'. He would never don gloves again. He had fallen out of love with boxing and wanted to return home to Belfast. He approached the management of ICI in Manchester and explained his predicament. They were sympathetic and arranged for John to be transferred to their Kilroot factory near Belfast, where the real business of family living could resume.

THE FORGOTTEN MAN
OF IRISH SPORT

The Irish forgive their great men when they are safely buried.
— Proverb

The Belfast to which John McNally returned in 1961 was a city that had acquired a new generation of boxing heroes. Both Johnny Caldwell and Freddie Gilroy – Olympic bronze medallists in 1956 – were setting the pace in the paid ranks. The King's Hall was doing a roaring trade, with both boxers filling it on a regular basis. In October 1962 the two were to clash in what was the high point of Belfast's professional boxing history. The meeting of Caldwell and Gilroy captured the imagination of the city as they met for Gilroy's British and Empire bantamweight titles in the King's Hall. The prize at stake – in theory – was a crack at the Brazilian world champion Eder Jofre. A record crowd of 15,000 from all classes and creeds packed in that evening to witness a fierce and bloodthirsty encounter. History shows that Gilroy was the victor that night when Caldwell retired in the ninth round, but John McNally was now a mere spectator in the King's Hall, and one of an ever-growing band of forgotten ex-boxers.

McNally was making a good living as a supervisor in the Kilroot plant of ICI. However, in 1963 he agreed to look after the preparations of the best prospect that Ireland had in amateur terms. Jim McCourt

153

from Leeson St. was another product of the Immaculata club. He was setting the local scene alight with his classy style of boxing. He was untouchable in the ring – but temperamental. A disagreement with the Immaculata had left him in need of a trainer as the Tokyo Olympics drew near. Naturally, there was only one man living in the Falls district that could steer McCourt to the Tokyo Games in 1964 – John McNally agreed to look after the lightweight's training and preparation. The Helsinki silver medallist introduced an austere regime, which saw McCourt in the Belfast Hills each morning, and sparring two opponents simultaneously in the ring to sharpen up. By the time the Irish team was chosen for Tokyo, McCourt was first choice as lightweight as he had swept all his challengers aside. At the Games, McCourt was considered unlucky to lose his semi-final to the crack Russian Velikton Barannikov, who lost in the final to the Pole Jozef Grudzien. McCourt's bronze medal was quite an achievement for Ireland, and it was with John McNally's experience and advice that the Leeson St. boy came good.

At this stage, John found a new hobby – one that would prove a turning point in his life. There was a great musical tradition in St Peter's parish of Belfast and many fine exponents of music and song had been produced over the years. John was attracted to music through his association with a local band of 'black and white minstrels', and it was not long until he was learning – and then playing – the banjo and mandolin with the group. One thing led to another and in the late 1960s the band The Freemen were formed. The group were fine exponents of Irish folk music and toured the world, with John at the helm. The band recorded many albums and inspired scores of other musicians in Belfast and further a field with their distinct style. John soon left ICI as the band became a lucrative business in itself. The good times in the music business continued for twenty years until the band came to a natural end. John's love of boxing waned and his achievements as an amateur became lost in the mists of time. John McNally and his five children eventually moved to the Hillhead district of Andersonstown, where he remained an unassuming character: few knew anything of his boxing career.

In boxing and sporting terms, John McNally's life continued in a rather non-descript manner. From the day and hour he hung up his gloves, his achievement as Ireland's first Olympic boxing medallist went largely unrecognised. On an official level, Belfast never marked the achievement of the man who brought home the city's first Olympic medal. Northern Ireland, as an entity, overlooked the man who had won the country's first Olympic medal. It is a sad indictment of so many so-called 'great and good' that a truly historic achievement never got the recognition it deserved.

The writer Cathal O'Byrne – author of the definitive social history of Belfast *As I Roved Out* – said of the city that it was a place that 'dearly loved a lord'. Linenopolis, as it was known, its bridges, buildings, monuments and thoroughfares are named after an assortment of lords and ladies, dukes, knights, earls and other such titled notables. Prince Albert, the Consort of Queen Victoria, who died in 1851, is celebrated in Belfast by a bridge, a clock, a quay, a court, a terrace, a street and, if that was not enough, there is a road named after his bridge. For a German Prince whose personal link to Belfast was tenuous, this is quite an achievement. However, John McNally, like a wealth of other Belfast notables, is just another uncelebrated citizen of the city. In John McNally's wake, five other Belfast boxers won Olympic medals. Names such as John Caldwell, Freddie Gilroy, Jim McCourt, Hugh Russell and Wayne McCullough all put Belfast on the sporting map – the city's Olympic boxing pedigree is truly astounding.

It cannot be denied that John McNally was a truly cracking amateur, whose class shone for only a sadly short period. Nevertheless, what a period it was! Three American Golden Gloves champions, three German champions and the cream of Olympians all fell to unanimous decisions. The final question as to who would have been bantamweight champion in 1952 if the Olympic Games had not been held in Finland, is open to question. John McNally's name is – and will always be – in the record books as the first man to bring an Olympic medal to Belfast and Northern Ireland, and a boxing medal to the island of Ireland. That achievement can never be denied and while his name is still in the collective folk memory, perhaps it is time that something was done to acknowledge this oversight.

EPILOGUE

On Friday 4 January 2008, the Irish Amateur Boxing Association inducted John McNally into its Hall of Fame. At a star-studded event held at the National Stadium in Dublin, the Olympian received a standing ovation as RTÉ's Jimmy Magee paid tribute to his achievement. McNally was described by Magee as the 'Pathfinder' of Irish boxing, who had inspired many generations to glory by his feat in Helsinki. Fifty-six years after the glory of Helsinki, John McNally's name was finally added to the list of the greatest in Irish boxing.

INDEX TO OTHER BOXERS

Index to Other Boxers